Senior Editor	Angela Crawley
Designer	Siân Williams
Editor-in-Chief	John Grisewood
Design Director	Paul Wilkinson
Consultant Editor	John Bollard
Cartoon Illustrations	Rachel Conner (Linda Rogers Associates)
Photography	Tim Ridley, Nick Goodall
Additional Design	Smiljka Surla
Additional Artwork Preparation	Julian Ewart, Matthew Gore, Simon Paine, Terry Parker, Janet Woronkowicz
Prop Organizers	Katxu Alexander, Karen Fielding
Artwork Archivists	Wendy Allison, Steve Robinson
Artwork Researcher	Caleb Cobell
DTP Operators	Tracey McNerney, Nina Tara
Production Manager	Susan Latham
Production Assistant	Selby Sinton

KINGFISHER
Larousse Kingfisher Chambers Inc.
95 Madison Avenue
New York, New York 10016

First American edition 1995
4 6 8 10 9 7 5   (HC)
4 6 8 10 9 7 5   (RLB)

LIBRARY OF CONGRESS CATALOGING-IN-PUBLICATION DATA
The Kingfisher first dictionary/edited by John Grisewood, Angela Crawley.—1st American ed.
p. cm.
1. English language—Dictionaries, Juvenile. [1. English
language—Dictionaries.] J. Grisewood, John. II. Crawley, Angela.
PE1628.5.K53 1995
423—dc20 94-47819 CIP AC

ISBN 1-85697-577-0 (HC)
ISBN 1-85697-641-6 (RLB)

Printed in Hong Kong

About this dictionary

The Kingfisher First Dictionary has been specially written and illustrated for children who are learning to read. The words in the dictionary have been carefully selected from those that young children see and use every day. As well as being easy to use and fun to browse through, this dictionary will help children develop the skills that will eventually enable them to become confident users of adult dictionaries. Younger children will enjoy looking at the colorful pictures and matching them with the words; older children will have fun consulting the dictionary for meanings and spellings.

This dictionary has a number of key features which combine to make it an indispensable learning tool:

▷ **Definitions** are carefully written in clear, simple English. **Example sentences** show how to use many of the words, and the attractive **illustrations** and **photographs** help to clarify the meaning of words.

▷ The bright **picture pages**, on topics such as shapes, animals, and cars, will reinforce the meaning and spelling of familiar words and broaden the young reader's vocabulary.

▷ **Wordplay** boxes encourage the child to make active use of the dictionary in order to solve a variety of word games and puzzles, thereby developing important word skills and building confidence by using a dictionary.

Occasional **Word origin** boxes provide a first entertaining insight into the way certain words have come about.

Simple **spelling tips** alert children to words that sound the same and help to guide them to the place in the dictionary where they will find the word they are looking for.

Contents

▷ The **More about words** section at the back of the book explains nouns, pronouns, verbs, helping verbs, contractions, adjectives, adverbs, prepositions, conjunctions, and articles.

Using your dictionary

The **letter string** on every page helps you to remember the order of the alphabet and to find the word you are looking for more quickly.

Pictures and photographs help you to understand the meanings of words.

If a word has more than one meaning, each meaning has a number before it.

Here you can see how to use the word in a sentence.

> **note**
>
> **1** A **note** is a short letter to somebody. *The note says Sarah has gone swimming.*
> **2** A **note** is also one sound in music.

> **goose** (geese)

For some words, there is a special way of talking about more than one of the thing, so we say one **goose** but two **geese** (not two **gooses**). These special words are shown in the dictionary.

The dictionary also tells you how to say words that have difficult spellings.

> **rough** *say ruff

> **geese** Look at **goose**.

If you look up **geese** in the dictionary, it tells you that you need to look at **goose** to find the word explained.

This dictionary shows you the special ways of writing a word that tell you about when something happened:

Emma is **drinking** a glass of water now.

Emma **drank** three glasses of water this morning.

Some words change their spelling when they are used in different ways: *I have a **big** present, Joe's is **bigger**, and Mia's is the **biggest**.* The dictionary lists these spellings.

> **drink** (drinking, drank, drunk)

Emma has **drunk** a lot of water today!

> **big** (bigger, biggest)

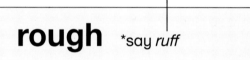

above

Above means higher than something. *Your nose is **above** your mouth.*

accident

An **accident** is something bad that happens which nobody has planned.

*Amy's dad had a car **accident**.*

ache *say ake

An **ache** is a pain in your body that goes on hurting, like an **earache**.

acorn

An **acorn** is the nut that grows on an oak tree.

acrobat

An **acrobat** is a person who can do difficult balancing tricks.

across

Across means from one side to the other. *There is a bridge **across** the river.*

act (acting, acted)

If you **act** in a play, you take part in it. *Aziz **acted** in the school play.* A person who **acts** is an **actor**.

add (adding, added)

If you **add** numbers, you put them together.

*If you **add** three and two, you get five.*

address (addresses)

Your **address** is the number or name of the building where you live and the name of the street and town where it is.

Patricia Ramos
8848 First Avenue
St. James City
Florida 33956
U.S.A.

adult

An **adult** is a grown-up. When children grow up, they become **adults**.

adventure

An **adventure** is an exciting or dangerous thing that happens to you. *I am reading a book about the **adventures** of three children who got lost in the jungle.*

affection

Affection is a tender love for someone.

afford

If you can **afford** something, you have enough money to buy it. *Can you **afford** to buy your brother a present?*

afraid

If you are **afraid**, you think something bad will happen to you.

*Are you **afraid** of spiders?*

after

After means at a later time. *I am going to my friend's house **after** school.*

afternoon

The **afternoon** is the part of the day between morning and evening. *We come home from school at three in the **afternoon**.*

again

Again means once more. *Sing that song again.*

age

Your **age** is the number of years you have lived. Your **age** changes every time you have a birthday. *Richard and his friends are all different **ages**.*

agree (agreeing, agreed)

If you **agree** with somebody, you think the same about something. *My sister thinks this is a good book, but I don't agree with her.*

air

We breathe **air**. It is all around us, and birds and aircraft fly in it.

aircraft (aircraft)

An **aircraft** is any machine that flies. Helicopters, gliders, and airplanes are **aircraft**. (Look at the next page.)

airplane

An **airplane** is a machine that flies. It has wings and an engine.

alike

If two people or things are **alike**, they are the same in some way. *Amy and Becky look alike because they are twins.*

alive

A person, an animal, or a plant that is **alive** is living now. *Plants must have water to stay alive.*

all

All means every one or every part of something. *All the puppies are brown.*

alligator

An **alligator** is an animal with sharp teeth and a long tail. It lives in rivers in some hot countries. **Alligators** are reptiles.

allow (allowing, allowed)

When somebody **allows** you to do something, they let you do it. *My dad sometimes allows me to use his computer.*

Wordplay
How many words can the ape make by adding one letter at a time to the beginning of **all**?

Answers at the back!

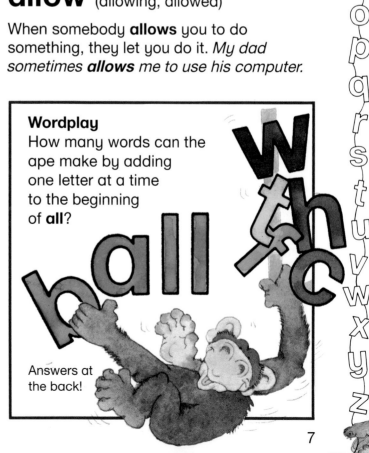

Aircraft

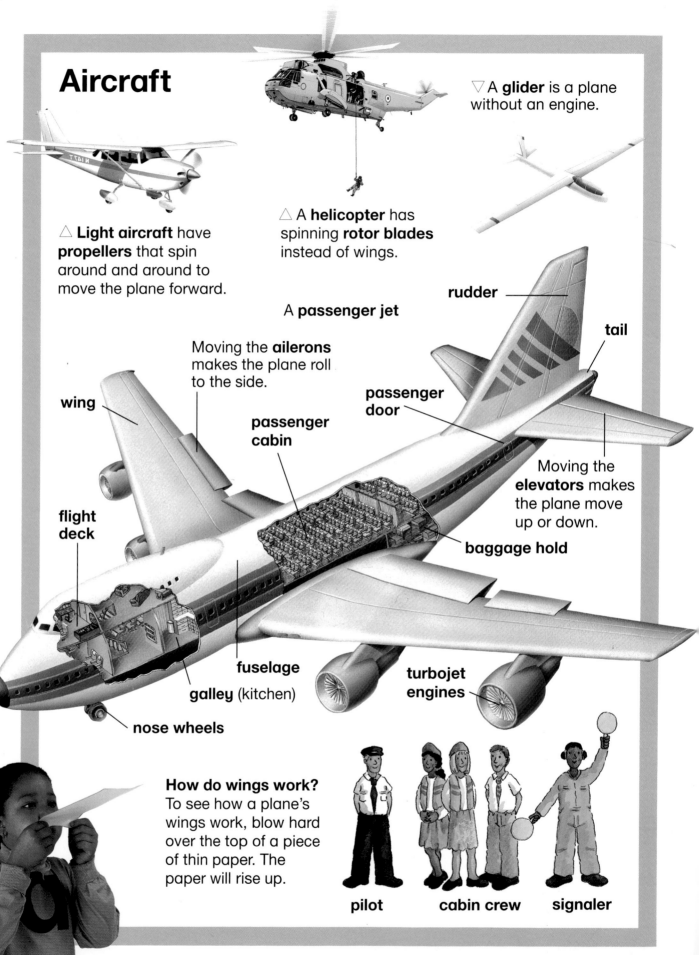

▽ A **glider** is a plane without an engine.

△ **Light aircraft** have **propellers** that spin around and around to move the plane forward.

△ A **helicopter** has spinning **rotor blades** instead of wings.

A **passenger jet**

rudder

tail

Moving the **ailerons** makes the plane roll to the side.

wing

passenger door

passenger cabin

Moving the **elevators** makes the plane move up or down.

flight deck

baggage hold

fuselage

galley (kitchen)

turbojet engines

nose wheels

How do wings work?
To see how a plane's wings work, blow hard over the top of a piece of thin paper. The paper will rise up.

pilot

cabin crew

signaler

a
b
c
d
e
f
g
h
i
j
k
l
m
n
o
p
q
r
s
t
u
v
w
x

almost

Almost means nearly, or not quite. *Ned can **almost** touch his toes.*

alone

When you are **alone**, you are not with anybody else. *I like to be **alone** when I am reading.*

along

Along means from one end of something to the other end. *There are trees **along** the riverbank.*

aloud

Aloud means not silently. *Read your poem **aloud** so everybody can hear.*

Another word that sounds like **aloud** is **allowed**.

alphabet

The **alphabet** is all the letters that we use to write words, from A to Z.

You can see the **alphabet** at the side of this page.

Alpha and **beta** are the first two letters of the Greek alphabet. Put together, they make the word **alphabet**.

always

Always means all the time or every time. *It is **always** dark at night. I **always** go to bed before my brother.*

ambulance

An **ambulance** is a large car or van for taking people who are sick or hurt to the hospital.

amount

An **amount** of something is how much there is. *I get the same **amount** of spending money as my sister.*

amphibian

Amphibians are animals that can live on land and in water. Frogs and toads are **amphibians**.

angry (angrier, angriest)

If somebody is **angry**, they are mad. *Dad was **angry** when my brother broke the window.*

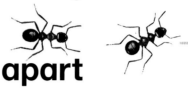

animal

An **animal** is anything that is living and can move around. Cats, whales, bees, and fish are **animals**, but trees are not.

ankle

Your **ankle** is the part of your leg where it joins your foot.

annoy (annoying, annoyed)

If you **annoy** somebody, you make them angry. *Ella is **annoyed** with me because I am late.*

another

Another means one more. *May I have **another** piece of paper?*

answer

1 (answering, answered) When you **answer**, you speak to somebody who has called you or asked you a question.
2 An **answer** is what you say when somebody asks you a question.

ant

An **ant** is a tiny insect. **Ants** live in nests under the ground.

apart

1 Apart means away from each other. *Stand with your legs **apart**.*
2 If you take something **apart**, it is in pieces. *John took the lamp **apart** to see if he could fix it.*

ape

An **ape** is an animal like a big monkey without a tail. Orangutans are **apes**.

apologize (apologizing, apologized)

When you **apologize**, you say you are sorry for something that you have done.

appear (appearing, appeared)

When something **appears**, you can suddenly see it. *The Sun **appeared** from behind a cloud.*

apple

An **apple** is a round fruit with a green, red, or yellow skin. **Apples** grow on trees.

Animals

A **toucan** is a **bird**.

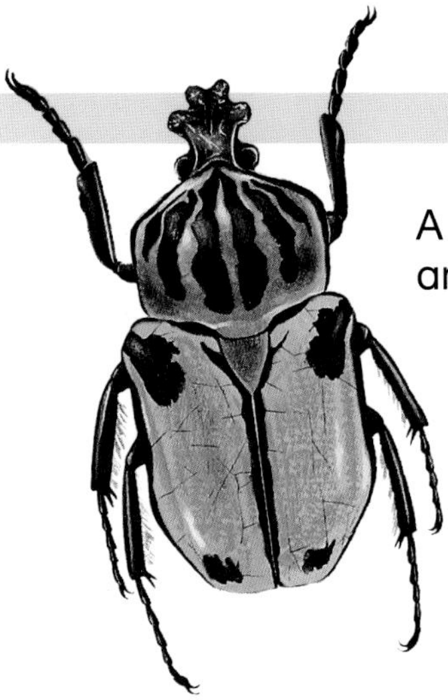

A **beetle** is an **insect**.

A **goldfish** is a **fish**.

A **toad** is an **amphibian**.

A **rabbit** is a **mammal**.

A **turtle** is a **reptile**.

Some other groups of animals

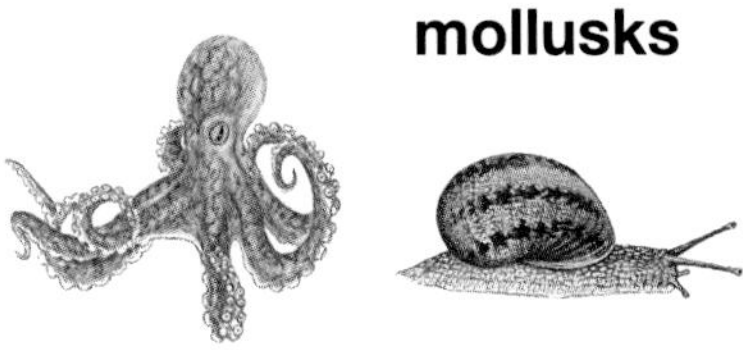

mollusks

spiders

crustaceans

insect   bird   amphibian   mammal   fish   reptile

Animal groups
Do you know what these animals are called? Which groups do they belong to?
Answers at the back!

a b c d e f g h i j k l m n o p q r s t u v w x y z

area

An **area** is a part of a country or a place. *We don't live in this **area**.*

argue (arguing, argued)

If you **argue** with somebody, you talk in an angry way because you do not agree about something.

arm

Your **arms** are the parts of your body between your hands and your shoulders.

armor

Armor is a strong metal covering that soldiers used to wear to protect their bodies.

army (armies)

An **army** is a large group of soldiers who fight together.

around

Around means on all sides of something. *There is a fence **around** the field.*

arrive (arriving, arrived)

If you **arrive** somewhere, you get there. *What time does the train **arrive**?*

arrow

1 An **arrow** is a thin stick with a point at one end. You shoot **arrows** with a bow.
2 An **arrow** is also a sign that points to tell you the way.

art

Art is something beautiful that somebody has made, like a painting or a statue.

artist

An **artist** is a person who draws or paints pictures or makes other beautiful things.

ask (asking, asked)

1 When you **ask** a question, you are trying to get an answer. *"Where is the nearest post office?" she **asked**.*
2 When you **ask** for something, you say that you would like it. *I **asked** for a drink.*

asleep

When you are **asleep**, you are sleeping. *Katie is **asleep**.*

astronaut

Astronaut is made from two Greek words that mean "star" and "sailor." So an astronaut is somebody who sails toward the stars!

An **astronaut** is a person who travels in space.

ate Look at **eat**.

atlas
(atlases)

An **atlas** is a book of maps.

attic

An **attic** is a room or space at the top of a house under the roof.

attract (attracting, attracted)

When something **attracts** people or things, it makes them come closer.

audience

An **audience** is a group of people watching or listening to something like a play or film.

aunt

Your **aunt** is the sister of your father or your mother, or the wife of your uncle.

automobile

An **automobile** is a car. This word is sometimes shortened to **auto**.

autumn

Autumn is the part of the year that comes after summer. Leaves drop off the trees in **autumn**. Another word for **autumn** is fall.

awake

When you are **awake**, you are not asleep. *Katie is still in bed, but she is **awake**.*

awful

If something is **awful**, it is very, very bad. *This medicine tastes **awful**.*

ax

An **ax** is a tool with a long handle and a sharp blade. People use **axes** to cut wood.

Bb

baby (babies)

A **baby** is a very young child.

back

1 Your **back** is the part of your body behind you, between your neck and your bottom.
2 Back is the opposite of front. *Mom and Dad sat in the front of the car and I sat in the back.*

backward

If you say the alphabet **backward**, you start with Z and finish with A. *I am walking backward, so I can't see where I'm going.*

bad (worse, worst)

1 Bad means not good. *Eating lots of chocolate is bad for you.*
2 Food that is **bad** is too old to eat. *This egg has gone bad—it smells terrible!*

bag

You put things in a **bag** so you can carry them. **Bags** are made of plastic, paper, leather, or cloth. *We put the cookies in a bag.*

bake (baking, baked)

You **bake** food by cooking it in an oven. *I am baking a cake for Jo's birthday.*

balance
(balancing, balanced)

When you **balance**, you keep steady without falling. *Jenny is balancing on one leg.*

ball

A **ball** is a round thing that you use in games. *Throw the ball and I will try to catch it.*

ballet *say ba**lay**

Ballet is a kind of dance.

balloon

A **balloon** is a kind of bag made of thin rubber or plastic. You fill a **balloon** with air or gas to make it float.

banana

A **banana** is a long fruit with a yellow skin.

band

1 A **band** is a group of people who play music together.
2 A **band** is also a thin piece of material around something. *Put a rubber band around the letters to keep them together.*

bandage

A **bandage** is a clean strip of white cloth. You wrap a **bandage** around a cut on your body to keep it safe and clean.

bank

1 A **bank** is a place that looks after money for people.
2 A **bank** is also the land along the sides of a river.

bar

1 A **bar** is a long piece of metal.
2 A **bar** is also a piece of something hard, like chocolate or soap.

bare

1 **Bare** means without any clothes on. *Ned is walking around with bare feet.*
2 **Bare** also means empty. *Our house would look very bare without any furniture.*

Another word that sounds like **bare** is **bear**.

bark

1 (barking, barked) When a dog **barks**, it makes a loud sound.
2 **Bark** is the rough outside of a tree trunk.

barn

A **barn** is a building on a farm where the farmer keeps animals and things like hay. *The horses sleep in the barn.*

base

The **base** of something is the part at the bottom that it stands on. *The lamp has a flat base.*

baseball

Baseball is a game played by two teams with a bat and a ball.

basket

You can put things in a **basket** to carry them. **Baskets** are usually made of thin sticks or straw.

*Jason is carrying a **basket** of fruit.*

basketball

Basketball is a game played by two teams with a large ball. The players try to throw the ball into a high net.

bat

1 A **bat** is an animal like a mouse with wings. **Bats** fly at night.

2 A **bat** is also something that you use for hitting the ball in games like baseball and softball.

bathtub

A **bathtub** is a large container for water. You sit or lie in it to wash your whole body.

battery (batteries)

A **battery** is something that stores electricity. You put **batteries** in things like radios and watches to make them work.

beach (beaches)

A **beach** is a place next to the sea that is covered with sand or stones.

beak

A **beak** is the hard, pointed part of a bird's mouth.

bear

A **bear** is a large, wild animal with thick fur.

Another word that sounds like **bear** is **bare**.

beard

A **beard** is the hair that grows on a man's chin. *My uncle has grown a **beard**.*

beat (beating, beat, beaten)

If you **beat** somebody in a game or a race, you win.

beautiful

Something that is **beautiful** is lovely to look at, to hear, or to smell. *Those flowers are beautiful.*

beaver

A **beaver** is a furry animal that lives in and by rivers. **Beavers** have strong, sharp front teeth and a flat tail for swimming.

bed

You lie on a **bed** when you sleep.

bee

A **bee** is a flying insect that makes honey.

beetle

A **beetle** is an insect with hard wings.

before

1 **Before** means at an earlier time. *I have breakfast **before** I go to school.*
2 **Before** also means in front of somebody or something. *A comes **before** B in the alphabet.*

begin (beginning, began, begun)

When something **begins**, it starts. *What time does the movie **begin**?*

behave (behaving, behaved)

If you **behave** yourself, you are good and you do what somebody has told you to do.

behind

Behind means at the back of something. *Billy is hiding **behind** the tree.*

believe (believing, believed)

1 If you **believe** something, you are sure that it is true. *Do you **believe** in ghosts?*
2 If you **believe** somebody, you are sure that they are telling the truth.

bell

A **bell** makes a ringing sound when you hit it or press it.

Wordplay
Can you find the words that sound the same?

son   nose   bear
two   I   meet
see   pair

too   sea
                pear
knows
         meat   eye
bare   sun

Answers at the back!

belong (belonging, belonged)

When something **belongs** to you, it is yours. *Does this pen **belong** to you?*

below

Below means under. *Your mouth is **below** your nose.*

belt

A **belt** is a long piece of cloth or leather that you can wear around your waist.

bend (bending, bent)

If you **bend** something, it is not straight anymore. *Amman is **bending** a piece of wire. Hugo is **bending** down to pick up his pencil.*

berry (berries)

A **berry** is a small, soft fruit with seeds in it.

beside

Beside means next to. *Bella is standing **beside** Billy.*

best

The **best** person or thing is better than all the others. *This is the **best** ice cream I have ever tasted*!

better

1 Better is the way to say "more good" or "more well." *Apples are **better** for you than candy. I can draw **better** than my sister.*
2 If you are feeling **better**, you are well again. *I had a cold last week, but I am feeling **better** now.*

between

Between means in the middle.

*Bella is standing **between** Aziz and Cara.*

*Tuesday comes **between** Monday and Wednesday.*

bicycle

A **bicycle** has two wheels and pedals. A **bicycle** is often called a **bike**.

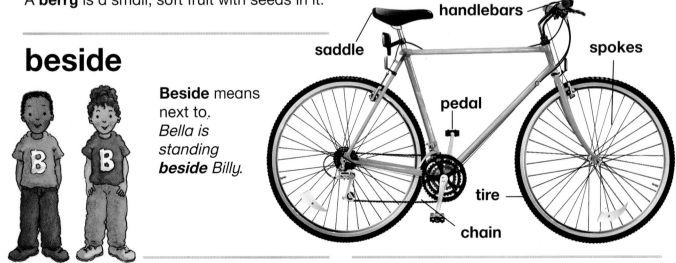

handlebars
saddle
spokes
pedal
tire
chain

big (bigger, biggest)

Big means not small. *This hat is too **big** for Saskia.*

bike Look at **bicycle**.

bird

Birds have wings and feathers. Most **birds** can fly. (Look at the next page.)

birthday (birthdays)

Your **birthday** is a special day every year. You remember it because you were born on that date. *My **birthday** is the first of May.*

biscuit

A **biscuit** is a small, light bread.

bite (biting, bit, bitten)

When you **bite** something, you cut into it with your teeth.

*Jenny is **biting** a carrot.*

blade

A **blade** is the flat, sharp part of a knife.

blame (blaming, blamed)

If you **blame** somebody for something bad that happened, you think they made it happen. *My brother **blamed** me for breaking his computer.*

blanket

A **blanket** is a warm, thick cover for a bed.

blew Look at **blow**.

blind

1 Somebody who is **blind** cannot see at all.
2 A **blind** is something that you pull down to cover a window.

blink (blinking, blinked)

When you **blink**, you close your eyes and then open them again quickly.

block

1 A **block** is a thick piece of something, like wood or stone, with straight sides.
2 (blocking, blocked) If something **blocks** a place, other people or things cannot get through.

*A fallen tree was **blocking** the road.*

Birds

▷ A **flamingo** has long legs for walking through deep water.

▷ An **eagle** has sharp claws called **talons** and a curved beak for tearing meat apart.

Feathers help to keep birds warm.

A bird has a hard **beak** or **bill** instead of teeth.

◁ **Ducks** paddle in the water with their **webbed feet**.

tail

wing

Birds have **claws** for holding onto things.

Birds build **nests** and lay their **eggs** there. The **chick** hatches out of the egg by cracking open the shell.

▷ **Parrots** have strong claws and short, curved beaks that they use for climbing around in trees.

◁ **Penguins** cannot fly, but they use their wings to help them swim.

blood

Blood is the red liquid that flows around inside your body.

blow (blowing, blew, blown)

1 When you **blow**, you push air out of your mouth. *April is blowing out the candles on the birthday cake.*
2 When the wind **blows**, the air moves.

boat

Boats carry people or things on water. A canoe is a kind of **boat**. Some **boats** have sails and some have engines. (Look at the next page.)

body (bodies)

Your **body** is the whole of you. People and animals have **bodies**. Your **body** can also be the whole of you apart from your head.

boil (boiling, boiled)

When water **boils**, it gets very hot. You can see bubbles in it and steam coming off it.

bone

Your **bones** are the hard parts inside your body. All your **bones** together are called a skeleton.

book

A **book** is pieces of paper joined together inside a cover. Most **books** have words and pictures inside them. You are reading a **book** at the moment.

boot

A **boot** is a kind of shoe that covers your foot and part of your leg. *My winter boots keep my feet very warm.*

bored

If you are **bored**, you feel tired and unhappy because you have nothing interesting to do.

born

When a baby is **born**, it starts to live outside its mother.

borrow (borrowing, borrowed)

If you **borrow** something from somebody, you take it for a short time and then you give it back. *I often borrow books from the library.*

both

Both means one and the other. *Toby and Hugo are both wearing red shirts.*

Boats

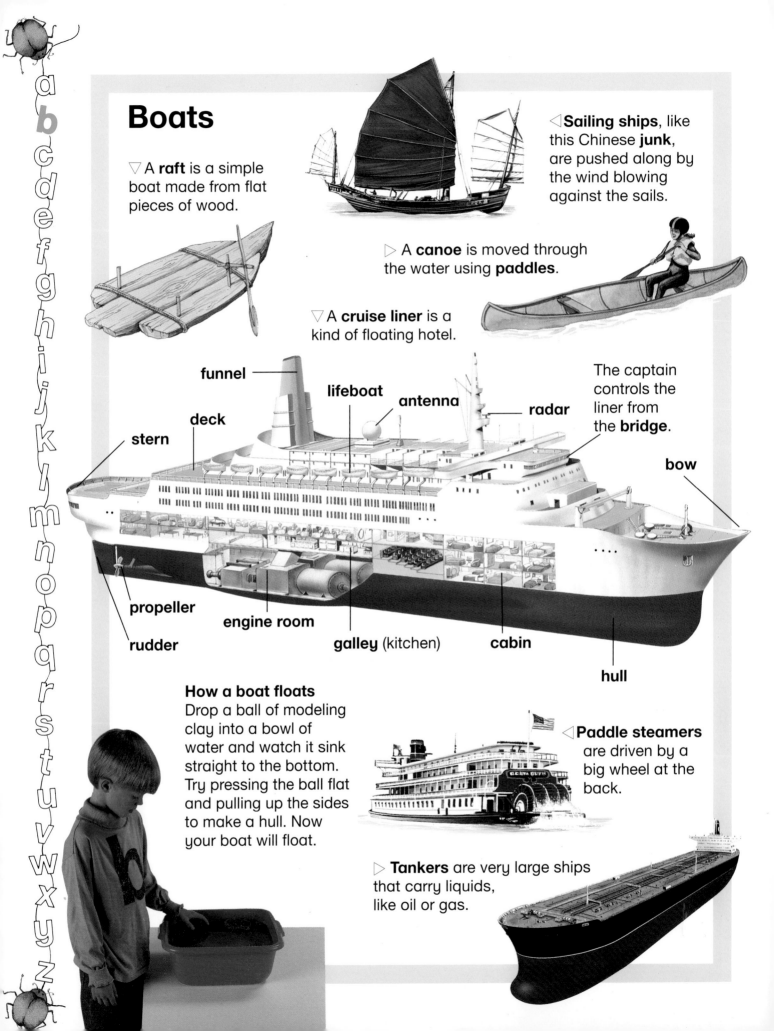

▽ A **raft** is a simple boat made from flat pieces of wood.

◁ **Sailing ships**, like this Chinese **junk**, are pushed along by the wind blowing against the sails.

▷ A **canoe** is moved through the water using **paddles**.

▽ A **cruise liner** is a kind of floating hotel.

The captain controls the liner from the **bridge**.

funnel

lifeboat

antenna

radar

deck

stern

bow

propeller

engine room

galley (kitchen)

cabin

rudder

hull

How a boat floats
Drop a ball of modeling clay into a bowl of water and watch it sink straight to the bottom. Try pressing the ball flat and pulling up the sides to make a hull. Now your boat will float.

◁ **Paddle steamers** are driven by a big wheel at the back.

▷ **Tankers** are very large ships that carry liquids, like oil or gas.

bottle

Bottles are tall containers that hold liquids. They are made of glass or plastic.

bottom

1 The **bottom** of something is its lowest part. *The ship sank to the **bottom** of the sea.*
2 Your **bottom** is the part of your body that you sit on.

bought Look at **buy**.

bounce (bouncing, bounced)

When a ball **bounces**, it springs up again after it hits the ground.

bow *rhymes with *so*

A **bow** is a kind of knot that you use to tie ribbon or string. *Can you tie your shoelaces in a **bow**?*

bow *rhymes with *now*
(bowing, bowed)

If you **bow**, you bend your body and head forward and down. *Actors **bow** at the end of a play.*

bowl

A **bowl** is a deep, round dish for food or liquids. *Barry poured soup into the **bowls**.*

box (boxes)

You use a **box** for keeping things in. **Boxes** have straight sides and they are usually made of cardboard or wood. *Naomi keeps all her toys in a toy **box**. You buy matches in a **matchbox**.*

boy (boys)

A **boy** is a male child who will grow up to be a man.

brain

Your **brain** is inside your head. It controls the rest of your body and you use it for thinking and feeling.

branch (branches)

A **branch** is one of the parts of a tree that grow out from the trunk. Leaves grow from the **branches**.

brave

If you are **brave**, you show that you are not afraid, even though something hurts or frightens you.

bread

Bread is food made from flour and baked in an oven. *May I have a slice of bread and butter, please?*

break (breaking, broke, broken)

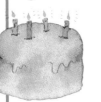

If you **break** something, it goes into pieces or it stops working. *I dropped my clock and broke it.*

Wordplay

All these things begin with **b**. What are they?

a part of a tree which grows out from the trunk

a special day every year that you remember because you were born on that day

a flower or leaf that is not open yet

an insect with hard wings

a small, light ball of soap or liquid with air inside

Now take the third letter of each of the words you found and mix them up to spell something beginning with **b** that you can see on some men's faces!
Answers at the back!

---

breakfast

Breakfast is the first meal of the day.

breathe (breathing, breathed)

When we **breathe**, we take air into our bodies through our noses and mouths and then let it out again.

brick

A **brick** is a block of baked clay. We use **bricks** for building.

bridge

A **bridge** is something that is built over a river or a road so that people can get from one side to the other.

bright

1 Bright lights shine very strongly. *The Sun is very bright today because there are no clouds in the sky.*
2 Bright colors are very clear and easy to see. *My bike is bright red.*
3 A person who is **bright** is smart.

bring (bringing, brought)

If you **bring** something, you carry it with you when you come. *I bring sandwiches with me to school every day.*

broke Look at **break**.

broken Look at **break**.

brother

Your **brother** is a boy who has the same mother and father as you.

brought Look at **bring**.

brush (brushes)

A **brush** is a tool that has a lot of stiff hairs joined to a handle. You use different kinds of **brushes** for doing different jobs. You make your hair neat with a **hairbrush** and you paint with a **paintbrush**.

bubble

A **bubble** is a small, light ball of soap or liquid with air inside.

*Hugo is blowing **bubbles**.*

bucket

You use a **bucket** for carrying things like liquids or sand. **Buckets** have handles and they are made of plastic or metal.

bud

A **bud** is a flower or a leaf that is not completely open.

build (building, built)

If you **build** something, you make it by putting parts together. *The **builders** are **building** a wall with bricks.*

building

Houses, schools, and hospitals are all **buildings**. A **building** has walls and a roof.

built Look at **build**.

bulb

1 A **bulb** is the glass part of a lamp.
2 A **bulb** is also the round root of a plant that grows under the ground. *Tulips grow from **bulbs**.*

bull

Cows and **bulls** are cattle. The **bull** is the male.

bulldozer

A **bulldozer** is a big, heavy machine that pushes dirt and rocks and makes land flat.

bunch (bunches)

A **bunch** is a group of things that are joined or tied together. *I gave Bella a **bunch** of flowers on her birthday. We ate a whole **bunch** of grapes.*

burn (burning, burned or burnt)

1 If something is **burning**, it is on fire.
2 If you **burn** something, you hurt or damage it with fire or heat. *Don't touch the stove or you will **burn** your hand.*

burst (bursting, burst)

If something **bursts**, it breaks open suddenly.

*If you stick a pin in a balloon, it will **burst**.*

bus (buses)

A **bus** is a big machine that can carry a lot of people from place to place. It has four wheels and an engine.

bush (bushes)

A **bush** is a small tree with a lot of branches that grows close to the ground.

busy (busier, busiest) *say **bizzy***

1 If you are **busy**, you have a lot of things to do. *I can't help you now because I am too **busy**.*
2 If a place is **busy**, a lot of things are happening there.

*We live on a very **busy** street.*

butter

Butter is soft, yellow food that is made from cream and milk from a cow. You can spread it on bread or use it in cooking.

butterfly (butterflies)

A **butterfly** is an insect with four pretty wings. **Butterflies** grow from caterpillars.

button

A **button** is a small, round thing on clothes. You push it through a hole called a **buttonhole** to keep your clothes together.

buy (buying, bought)

When you **buy** something, you pay money so you can have it. *I have **bought** a present for my friend because it is her birthday tomorrow.*

Cc

caboose

A **caboose** is the last car on a freight train. It is used by the train workers.

cage

A **cage** is a box or a room with bars. Animals and birds are often kept in **cages**. *My hamster lives in a cage.*

cake

A **cake** is a food made with flour, eggs, butter, and sugar and baked in an oven. *My friend baked a cake for my birthday.*

calendar

A **calendar** is a list of all the days, weeks, and months of a year. You will find today's date on a **calendar**.

calf (calves)

A **calf** is a young cow or bull.

call (calling, called)

1 If you **call** somebody, you speak loudly so that they will come to you, or you telephone them.
2 When somebody is **called** something, they have that name. *My dog is called Poppy.*

calves Look at **calf**.

camel

A **camel** is a big animal that can carry people or things in hot, dry countries. Some **camels** have one hump on their backs, and some have two.

camera

You take photographs with a **camera**.

camp

A **camp** is a place where people live in tents or huts for a short time.

can

A **can** is a metal container. You sometimes buy food like soup and vegetables in **cans**. Some drinks also come in **cans**.

candy

Candy is a sweet food made with sugar or syrup and other flavors that tastes good to eat.

canoe

A **canoe** is a small, narrow boat. You use a paddle to move it along.

cap

1 A **cap** is a small, soft hat that fits close to your head.
2 A **cap** is also a small lid. *Somebody forgot to put the cap back on the toothpaste.*

car

A **car** is a machine that you ride in. It has four wheels and an engine to make it go.

card

A **card** is a piece of thick paper. On special days like birthdays, people send **cards** with pictures and words on them. You use other **cards** to play games.

cardboard

Cardboard is thick paper that does not bend easily. It is used to make boxes.

care (caring, cared)

If you **care** for somebody or something, you look after them well. *People who do not care for their pets properly are cruel.*

careful

If you are **careful**, you think about what you are doing so that you do it safely and well. *Be careful! Don't drop those glasses!*

carpenter

A **carpenter** builds houses and furniture with wood.

carrot

A **carrot** is a long, orange-colored vegetable that grows under the ground.

carry (carries, carrying, carried)

When you **carry** something, you pick it up and take it to another place.

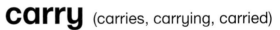

Ann is carrying some books.

Cars

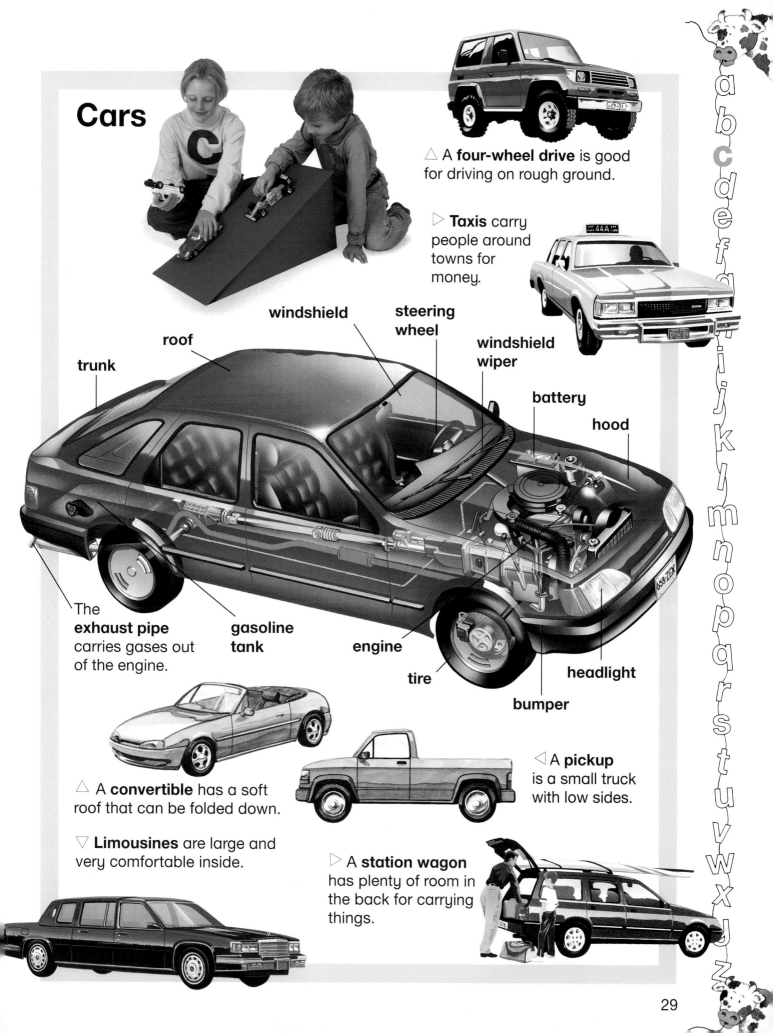

△ A **four-wheel drive** is good for driving on rough ground.

▷ **Taxis** carry people around towns for money.

roof

windshield

steering wheel

windshield wiper

battery

hood

trunk

The **exhaust pipe** carries gases out of the engine.

gasoline tank

engine

tire

bumper

headlight

△ A **convertible** has a soft roof that can be folded down.

▽ **Limousines** are large and very comfortable inside.

◁ A **pickup** is a small truck with low sides.

▷ A **station wagon** has plenty of room in the back for carrying things.

carton

A **carton** is a cardboard or plastic box. Food and drinks are packed in **cartons**.

cartoon

A **cartoon** is a short, funny movie using drawings, or a funny drawing in a newspaper.

cassette

A **cassette** is a plastic box with a tape inside it that stores sound and sometimes pictures.

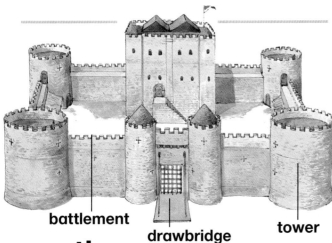

battlement   **drawbridge**   **tower**

castle

Castles were built long ago. They had thick high walls to keep the people inside safe from other people who wanted to attack them.

cat

A **cat** is a furry animal with sharp claws. People keep small **cats** as pets. A young **cat** is called a kitten. Large **cats**, like lions and tigers, live in the wild.

catch (catches, catching, caught)

1 When you **catch** somebody or something that is moving, you take hold of it. *If I throw the ball, will you catch it?*
2 When you **catch** an illness, you get it. *Cathy has caught a cold.*

caterpillar

Caterpillars look like furry worms with legs. They change into butterflies and moths.

cattle

Cattle are large animals that are kept on farms for their milk and meat. Cows and bulls are **cattle**.

caught Look at catch.

cause (causing, caused)

If you **cause** something, you make it happen.

cave

A **cave** is a big hole in the side of a mountain or under the ground. *People once lived in caves.*

ceiling

The **ceiling** is the top part of a room. *The lamp is hanging from the ceiling.*

center

The **center** of something is the middle part. *In the game, we all made a circle and Lucy stood in the center.*

century (centuries)

A **century** is a hundred years. *We are living at the end of the twentieth century.*

cereal

A **cereal** is a kind of food that we eat for breakfast. **Cereals** are made from the seeds of different plants, like rice and wheat.

chain

A **chain** is made of metal rings joined together.

chair

A **chair** is a seat with a back, for one person to sit on.

change (changing, changed)

1 When something **changes**, it becomes different. *Water changes into ice when it gets very cold.*
2 When you **change**, you put on different clothes. *Ann has to change before she can go to the party.*

chase (chasing, chased)

If you **chase** something or somebody, you go after them and try to catch them.

cheap

Something that is **cheap** does not cost a lot of money. *This toy car is very cheap.*

check (checking, checked)

When you **check** something, you look at it again to make sure that it is right. *Please check my spelling.*

cheek

Your **cheeks** are the soft parts on each side of your face.

cheerful

If you are **cheerful**, you feel happy.

cheese

Cheese is white or yellow food made from milk.

chest

1 A **chest** is a large strong box with a lid.
2 Your **chest** is the front part of your body between your neck and your stomach.

chew (chewing, chewed)

When you **chew** food, you use your teeth to make it soft. *The dog **chewed** my shoe.*

Wordplay
The word for more than one **child** is **children**. In this dictionary, you can see it written in brackets ( ) after the word **child**.

Do you know the word for more than one:

foot?

woman?

mouse?

calf?

city?

Use the dictionary to check your answers!

Answers at the back!

chick

A **chick** is a baby bird.

chicken

A **chicken** is a bird that lays the eggs we eat.

chief

A **chief** is the leader of a group of people. A **chief** tells other people what to do.

child (children)

A **child** is a boy or a girl. **Children** grow up to be men and women.

chimney (chimneys)

A **chimney** is a large pipe above a fire that lets smoke and gas go outside into the air.

chin

Your **chin** is the part of your face that is under your mouth.

chocolate

Chocolate is a sweet, brown food. It is used for making candy and cakes.

choose (choosing, chose, chosen)

When you **choose** something, you take it because it is the one you want. *Richard is choosing a new shirt.*

circle

A **circle** is a round shape, like a ring.

circus (circuses)

A **circus** is a group of people, like acrobats and clowns, that travels around giving shows in different places.

city (cities)

A **city** is a very big town. *Boston is a city.*

clap (clapping, clapped)

When you **clap**, you hit your hands together to make a loud noise. *We all clapped at the end of the play.*

class (classes)

A **class** is a group of pupils who are learning together at school. *There are thirty children in my class.*

claw

A **claw** is a sharp, curved nail on an animal's foot.

clay

Clay is a special kind of earth that becomes hard when it is dry. **Clay** is used for making things like bricks and pots.

clean

1 Something that is **clean** does not have any dirt or marks on it. *My hands are clean —I have just washed them.*
2 (cleaning, cleaned) When you **clean** something, you take away the dirt or marks. *I am cleaning my bike.*

clear

1 You can see through something that is **clear**. *Most glass is clear.*
2 If something is **clear**, it is easy to understand, to see, or to hear. *This photo isn't very clear because you moved the camera when you were taking it.*

Clothes

sleeve

tights

shorts

shirt

T-shirt

dress

collar

sweater

undershirt

blouse

button

underpants

pocket

belt

shoelace

cuff

jeans

shoes

skirt

socks

pajamas

bathrobe

hat

bathing suit

cap

scarf

coat

leotard

gloves

sweat suit

slippers

swimming trunks

boots

pants

sneakers

a b c d e f g h i j k l m n o p q r s t u v w x y z

clever

Somebody who is **clever** can learn and understand things quickly and well. *It was clever of you to do the puzzle so quickly.*

cliff

A **cliff** is a high hill with one side that goes straight down. *Many cliffs are by the sea.*

climb (climbing, climbed)

If you **climb** something, you move up using your hands and feet to hold on.

Jason is climbing the ladder.

clock

A **clock** is a machine that tells you what time it is.

close (closing, closed)
*say *klohz*

When you **close** something, you shut it. *Please close the door after you.*

close *say *klohs

Something that is **close** is near. *I live close to my school.*

closet

A **closet** is a small room for keeping things in.

cloth

Cloth is a material made out of thread. A lot of **cloth** is made of wool or cotton.

clothes

Your **clothes** are all the things you wear. Skirts, pants, and socks are **clothes**.

cloud

A **cloud** is millions of tiny drops of water that make a gray or white shape floating in the sky. *The water from clouds sometimes falls as rain.*

clown

A **clown** is a person who does funny things to make people laugh. **Clowns** paint their faces and dress up in strange clothes.

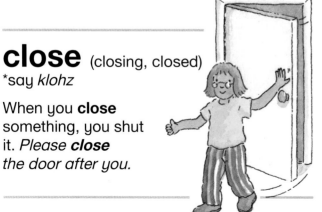

clue

A **clue** is something that helps to find the answer to a problem or mystery.

*The detective is looking for **clues** that will help him find the thief.*

coast

The **coast** is where the land meets the sea.

coat

You wear a **coat** on top of your other clothes to keep you warm on cold days.

cocoon

A **cocoon** is a small ball of threads made by a caterpillar. The caterpillar lives in the **cocoon** before it changes into a butterfly or a moth.

coffee

Coffee is a hot drink that is made by adding water to a brown powder. This powder is made from part of the **coffee** tree.

coin

A **coin** is a piece of money made of metal.

cold

1 Cold means not hot. Ice and snow are **cold**. *If you feel **cold**, put a sweater on.*

2 A **cold** is an illness. You sneeze when you have a **cold**.

collar

The **collar** of something like a shirt or a coat is the part that goes around your neck.

collect (collecting, collected)

When you **collect** things, you save up a lot of things because you are interested in them. *Charlie is **collecting** shells.*

color

Red, yellow, blue, and green are **colors**.

comfortable

Something that is **comfortable** is nice to be in or to wear. *I slept well because the bed is very **comfortable**.*

comic

A **comic** is a kind of magazine that tells stories in pictures.

Colors

Red, yellow, and blue are the **primary colors**. We mix these colors to make other colors.

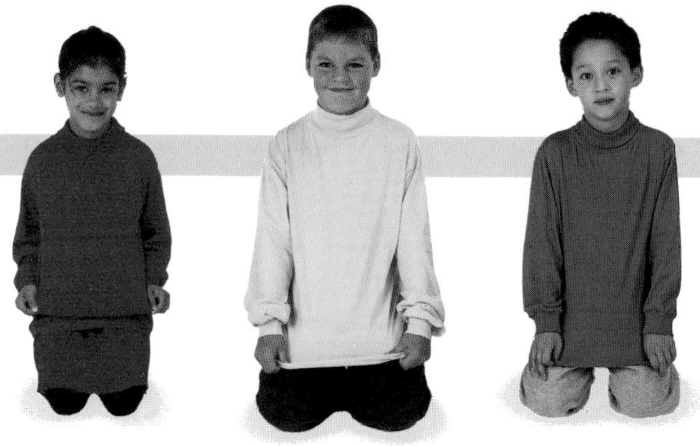

red   yellow   blue

Red and yellow make **orange**.

Yellow and blue make **green**.

pink

magenta

lilac

turquoise

lime green

olive green

gold

rust

brown

cream

Red and blue make **purple**.

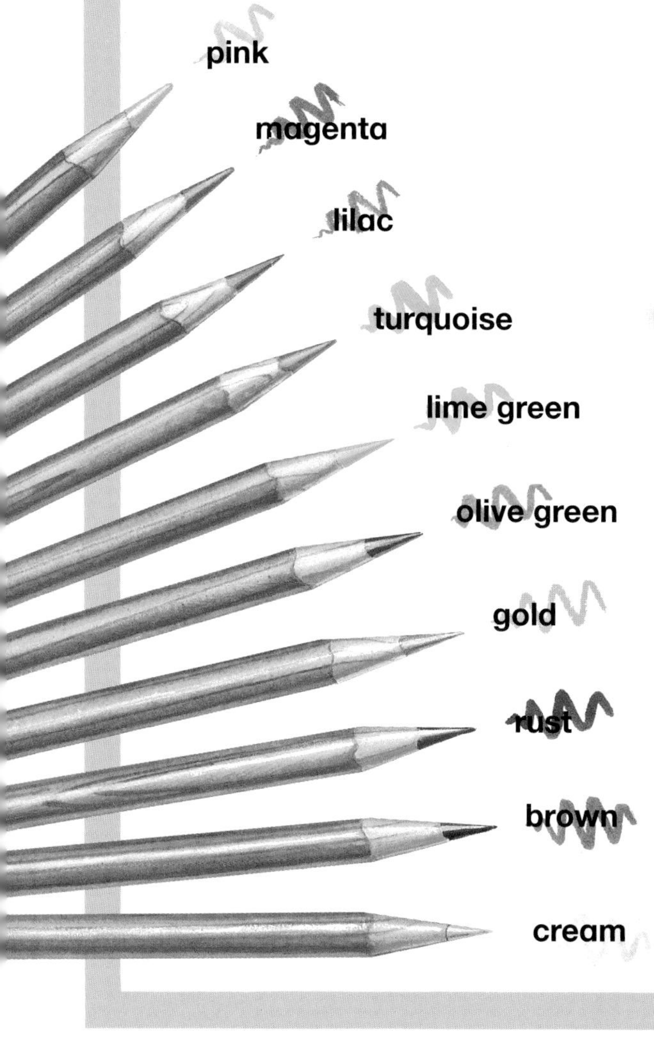

black

white

gray

pale blue

bright blue

dark blue

compact disc

A **compact disc** is a flat, round piece of silver-colored plastic that has music or words stored on it. We also call it a **CD**.

complete

If something is **complete**, it has no parts missing. *We saw a **complete** skeleton of a dinosaur in the museum.*

computer

A **computer** is a machine that can solve problems quickly, store information, and control other machines.

confuse (confusing, confused)

To **confuse** means to mix up somebody's ideas, so that they cannot understand. *My sister explained how to play the game, but she went too quickly and I got **confused**.*

container

A **container** is something for putting things in. Jars, bottles, and boxes are **containers**.

contest

A **contest** is way of finding out who is the best at doing something. *My brother won the spelling **contest** at school.*

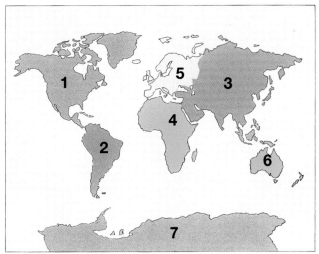

continent

The **continents** are the seven main areas of land of the world. They are **1** North America, **2** South America, **3** Asia, **4** Africa, **5** Europe, **6** Australia, and **7** Antarctica.

continue (continuing, continued)

When you **continue** doing something, you keep on doing it. *Matt **continued** watching television after his dad told him to go to bed.*

control (controlling, controlled)

If you **control** something, you make it do what you want. *She can't **control** her dog.*

cookie

A **cookie** is a small, sweet cake. **Cookies** are usually flat and crisp.

*My dad likes to bake **cookies** for us on Saturday afternoons.*

cool

If something is **cool**, it is a bit cold. *It was warm yesterday, but it is **cooler** today.*

copy (copying, copied)

When you **copy** something, you make it look or sound just like something else. *Ann's mom drew a picture of a horse, and Ann **copied** it.*

corn

Corn is a plant that farmers grow for its seeds, called kernels. Kernels of **corn** grow in rows on a **corncob**.

corner

A **corner** is a place where two roads, edges, or walls meet.

correct

If you are **correct**, you have not made a mistake.

cost (costing, cost)

The amount you pay for something is how much it **costs**. *How much did your new game **cost**?*

costume

A **costume** is all the clothes that an actor wears. *Katie is wearing a tiger **costume** for the school play.*

cotton

Cotton is the soft white hair on the seeds of a **cotton** plant. It is used for making cloth and thread.

cough *say koff (coughing, coughed)

When you **cough**, you make a sudden, loud noise in your throat.

Wordplay
Change the order of the letters to spell the names of six animals in this dictionary that begin with **c**.

tac

reoccolid

kichenc

falc

malec

piterlarcal

Answers at the back!

count (counting, counted)

When you **count**, you say numbers one after another in the right order. *Count from one to a hundred.* You also **count** when you add up a number of things. *Can you count how many stars there are in the sky?*

country (countries)

1 A **country** is a part of the world with its own people and laws. *Japan and Spain are countries.*

2 The **country** is the land outside towns where there are fields, woods, and farms. *We live in the country.*

cousin

Your **cousin** is the child of your uncle or aunt.

cover
(covering, covered)

When you **cover** something, you put something else over it to hide it or to keep it safe or warm.

*Alice is **covering** her teddy bear.*

cow

A **cow** is a large animal that gives us milk. A young **cow** is called a calf.

crack

A **crack** is a thin line on something where it is nearly broken. *There is a crack in this plate.*

crane

A **crane** is a tall machine that lifts and moves heavy things.

crash (crashes, crashing, crashed)

When something **crashes**, it hits something else with a very loud noise.

crawl (crawling, crawled)

When you **crawl**, you move along on your hands and knees.

a b c d e f g h i j k l m n o p q r s t u v w x y z

crayon

A **crayon** is a kind of soft pencil for drawing and coloring. **Crayons** are often made of wax.

cream

Cream is the thick part on the top of milk. *Would you like **cream** with your coffee?*

creature

A **creature** is any animal. *A dragon is a strange **creature** that you can read about in stories.*

creep (creeping, crept)

When you **creep**, you move quietly and slowly, trying not to be seen. *The cat is **creeping** toward the bird.*

cricket

1 A **cricket** is a jumping insect like a grasshopper. It makes a loud sound with its wings.
2 **Cricket** is also a game for two teams. It is played with a bat and ball.

cried Look at cry.

cries Look at cry.

crocodile

A **crocodile** is a large animal with a long body and big, sharp teeth. It lives in rivers in some hot countries. **Crocodiles** are reptiles.

crooked

Something that is **crooked** is not straight. *The old man's back was **crooked** so he had to walk with a cane.*

crop

Crops are plants that farmers grow as food.

cross

1 If you are **cross**, you feel angry about something.
2 (crosses, crossing, crossed) To **cross** means to go from one side to the other. *Look both ways before you **cross** the road.*
3 (crosses) A **cross** is a mark like + or X.

crowd

A **crowd** is a lot of people in one place. *I was looking for my friend in the **crowd**.*

a b c d e f g h i j k l m n o p q r s t u v w x y z

41

crown

A **crown** is a ring of gold and jewels that kings and queens wear on their heads.

cruel (crueller, cruellest)

Somebody who is **cruel** hurts other people or animals on purpose. *The witch in the story was very **cruel** to her cat.*

crumb

A **crumb** is a tiny bit of cake or bread.

cry (cries, crying, cried)

When you **cry**, you have tears falling from your eyes.

cub

A **cub** is a young bear, lion, tiger, fox, or wolf.

cube

A **cube** is a solid shape with six square sides. Dice are **cubes**.

cup

A **cup** is a small container with a handle. You drink things like tea and coffee from **cups**.

curl

A **curl** is a piece of hair in a curved shape. *Amman has **curly** hair.*

curtain

Curtains are pieces of cloth that you pull across a window to cover it.

curve (curving, curved)

When a line turns or bends one way, it **curves**.

*The letter C is a **curved** shape.*

cushion

A **cushion** is a bag filled with something soft. You put a **cushion** on a seat to make it more comfortable to sit on.

cut (cutting, cut)

You use scissors or a knife to **cut** things into pieces. *Jenny is **cutting** out a picture from her comic.*

Dd

daisy (daisies)

A **daisy** is a flower with white petals and a yellow middle.

damage (damaging, damaged)

If you **damage** something, you spoil or break it. *The building was badly **damaged** by the fire.*

damp

If something is **damp**, it is a little wet. *Your shirt isn't dry yet. It's still **damp**.*

dance
(dancing, danced)

When you **dance**, you move your body in time to music.

danger

When there is **danger**, something bad may happen.

*The sign said, "**Danger!** Keep out."*

dangerous

Something that is **dangerous** can hurt you. *It is **dangerous** to ride a bike at night without any lights.*

dark

1 Dark means without any light. *It is **dark** at night.*
2 Dark hair is brown or black.

date

The **date** is the day, the month, and sometimes the year when something happens. *Today's **date** is the thirteenth of June.*

daughter

Somebody's **daughter** is a girl or a woman who is their child.

day (days)

1 A **day** is a time of 24 hours. Every **day** starts at midnight and ends the next midnight. There are seven **days** in a week.
2 Day is also the time when it is light outside.

dead

A person, an animal, or a plant that is **dead** is not living anymore.

*This plant is **dead** because you forgot to water it.*

deaf

A person who is **deaf** cannot hear very well or cannot hear at all.

dear

1 You put **dear** before a person's name when you are writing a letter.
2 Something that is **dear** is important to you or someone else. *Our cat Binky is very **dear** to the family.*

Another word that sounds like **dear** is **deer**.

decide (deciding, decided)

When you **decide**, you make up your mind about something. *I can't **decide** which book to buy.*

deep

Something that is **deep** goes down a long way from the top. *When I can swim better, I will be able to go in the **deep** end of the pool with my sister.*

deer (deer)

Another word that sounds like **deer** is **dear**.

A **deer** is an animal that can run fast. **Deer** have long legs, and the males have big horns called antlers on their heads.

delicious

Something that is **delicious** is very good to eat. *This cake is **delicious**.*

deliver (delivering, delivered)

If somebody **delivers** something, they bring it to you. *The mail carrier **delivers** letters to our house every day.*

dentist

A **dentist** is a doctor who looks after people's teeth.

describe (describing, described)

When you **describe** somebody or something, you say what it is like. *Can you **describe** the place where you live?*

desert

A **desert** is very dry land where not many plants can grow.

design (designing, designed)

To **design** means to prepare a plan of something to show how it will be made. *At school we are designing all sorts of costumes for our play.*

desk

A **desk** is a kind of table with drawers. You can sit at a **desk** to read and write.

dessert

Dessert is any sweet food eaten after the main part of a meal. *Arnold had strawberries and cream for dessert.*

diamond

A **diamond** is a very hard jewel that looks like clear glass. *My mom's ring has a big diamond in it.*

diary (diaries)

A **diary** is a book where you write what happens every day. *I make notes about important things in my diary so that I don't forget about them.*

dice

Dice are small blocks made of wood or plastic with a different number of dots on each side. Just one of these is called a **die**.

dictionary (dictionaries)

A **dictionary** is a book where you can find what words mean and how to spell them. *You are reading a dictionary now.*

die (dying, died)

When a person, an animal, or a plant **dies**, it stops living. *We would all die without water.*

different

Different means not the same. *David and Tom's shirts are different colors. One is blue, and the other one is red.*

difficult

Something that is **difficult** is not easy to do. *That high wall would be very difficult to climb over.*

Dinosaurs

◁The sharp points on the end of **Stegosaurus**'s tail helped to protect it from attackers.

◁**Iguanodon** was a big and gentle plant eater.

▷ **Triceratops** used its big horns to frighten off meat eaters.

▽ **Apatosaurus** had a long neck so it could reach leaves at the tops of trees.

▽ Fierce **Velociraptor** had sharp claws and teeth and moved very fast.

▷ **Tyrannosaurus** had a huge mouth with very sharp teeth.

dig (digging, dug)

If you **dig**, you make a hole in the ground by moving soil or sand. You usually use a shovel for **digging**.

dinner

Dinner is the main meal of the day. Most people eat their **dinner** in the evening, but some people eat it in the middle of the day.

dinosaur

A **dinosaur** is an animal that lived millions of years ago. There were many different kinds of **dinosaur**.

> **Dinosaur** comes from two Greek words that mean "terrible lizard."

dip (dipping, dipped)

To **dip** means to put something in liquid, then quickly take it out again. *Flora **dipped** her finger in the cream and then tasted it.*

direction

A **direction** is the way that a person or thing is going. *We got lost because we went in the wrong **direction**.*

dirt

Dirt is mud, soil, or marks that must be cleaned off. *Our boots were covered in **dirt** after our walk in the fields, so we took them off before we went into the house.*

dirty (dirtier, dirtiest)

Something that is **dirty** is covered with dirt or marks. *My white pants got **dirty** when I sat down on the ground. Please go and wash your **dirty** hands.*

disappear (disappearing, disappeared)

When something **disappears**, it suddenly goes away. *The magician made the rabbit **disappear**.*

disappointed

If you are **disappointed**, you are unhappy because something you were hoping for did not happen. *I was **disappointed** when we couldn't go to the fair.*

discover (discovering, discovered)

When you **discover** something, you find out about it or you see it for the first time. *We **discovered** a secret hiding place in the hollow trunk of a tree.*

disguise

A **disguise** is something that you do to change the way you look, so that other people will not know who you are.

dish (dishes)

You use a **dish** for cooking food or putting it on the table. *We put the fruit salad in a big dish.*

distance

The **distance** between two places is how far they are from each other. *The distance between the swimming pool and my school is three miles.*

disturb (disturbing, disturbed)

If somebody **disturbs** you, they stop you doing what you are doing at the moment.

Please don't disturb Jesse because he's trying to read.

dive (diving, dived)

If you **dive** into water, you jump in with your hands and head first.

divide (dividing, divided)

1 When you **divide** something, you make it go into smaller parts. *Our teacher divided us into two teams for the game.*
2 When you **divide** numbers, you see how many times one number will go into another. *Eight divided by four is two.*

doctor

A **doctor** is a person who helps you to get better when you are sick.

dog

A **dog** is an animal that people keep as a pet. **Dogs** are also used to do work like guarding buildings or hunting. A young **dog** is called a puppy.

doll

A **doll** is a toy that looks like a small person.

dolphin

A **dolphin** is an animal that lives in the sea. **Dolphins** look like fish, but they are really mammals.

donkey (donkeys)

A **donkey** is an animal that looks like a small horse with long ears.

door

You open a **door** when you go in and out of a room or a building.

dot

A **dot** is a small, round spot, like this: ●

down

Down means from a higher to a lower place. *We ran down the hill.*

drag (dragging, dragged)

If you **drag** something, you pull it along slowly. *Katie is dragging her schoolbag along behind her.*

dragon

A **dragon** is an animal that you can read about in stories. **Dragons** have wings and long tails. Their bodies are covered in scales and they breathe fire.

drank Look at drink.

Wordplay
Trace this puzzle, then join the dots by following the letters in the order that they come in the alphabet to see a picture of something beginning with **d**.

Answer at the back!

draw
(drawing, drew, drawn)

If you **draw**, you make a picture with a pencil, pen, or crayon. *Thomas is **drawing** a picture of his family.*

drawer

A **drawer** is a box that you can push into and pull out of a piece of furniture. *I keep my socks in the top **drawer** and my shirts in the bottom **drawer**.*

drawing

A **drawing** is a picture that you make with a pencil, pen, or crayon.

Wordplay
How many little words can you find inside this word, keeping the letters in the same order?

Answers at the back!

drawn Look at **draw**.

dream (dreaming, dreamed or dreamt)

When you **dream**, pictures and thoughts go through your mind. You **dream** when you are asleep. *Last night I **dreamed** that I was flying like a bird.*

dress

1 (dresses) A **dress** is a skirt and top joined together. Girls and women wear **dresses**.
2 (dressing, dressed) When you get **dressed**, you put your clothes on. *In the mornings, I get up, brush my teeth, and then get **dressed**.*

drew Look at **draw**.

drill

A **drill** is a tool that you use for making holes. *The man is using an electric **drill** to make a hole in the wall.*

drink (drinking, drank, drunk)

When you **drink**, you take liquid into your body through your mouth.

*Emma is **drinking** a glass of water.*

drip (dripping, dripped)

When a liquid **drips**, it falls in small drops.
*Water is **dripping** through a hole in the roof.*

drive (driving, drove, driven)

To **drive** means to make something like a car or a bus move along. *My mom **drives** a bus. She's a bus **driver**.*

drop

1 (dropping, dropped)
If you **drop** something, you let it fall by accident. *She **dropped** a plate and it almost smashed.*
2 A **drop** of a liquid is a very small amount. *Rain is made of small **drops** of water.*

drove Look at drive.

drugstore

A **drugstore** is a store where you can buy medicine and other small things.

drum

A **drum** is a musical instrument that you hit with sticks or with your hands to make a sound.

drunk Look at drink.

dry

1 (drier, driest) Something that is **dry** is not wet. *You can't put your shirt on because it's not **dry** yet.*
2 (dries, drying, dried) When you **dry** something, you make it dry. *You **dry** yourself with a towel after a bath or shower.*

duck

A **duck** is a bird that can swim as well as fly. *We fed the **ducks** at the pond.*

dug Look at dig.

dull

Dull means not sharp. *My pencil was so **dull** that it would not write.*

dust

Dust is small bits of dry dirt that look like powder.

during

During means through the time of. *Owls sleep **during** the day.*

dying Look at die.

early (earlier, earliest)

1 Early means near the beginning of something. *The birds start singing early in the morning.*
2 Early also means before the usual time. *We arrived at the show early so we could get the best seats.*

earn (earning, earned)

To **earn** means to get money for work that you do. *Karen sometimes earns money by taking her neighbor's dog for walks.*

each

Each means every thing or every person. *The teacher gave each child a piece of paper and asked them to draw a picture.*

earth

1 We all live on a planet called **Earth**. Our **Earth** moves around the Sun.
2 The ground that plants grow in is also called **earth**. *In spring we dig the earth and plant seeds in it.*

eagle

An **eagle** is a large bird with a sharp, curved beak. **Eagles** catch and eat small animals and other birds.

earthquake

An **earthquake** happens when part of the ground suddenly begins to shake. **Earthquakes** sometimes make buildings fall down.

ear

People and animals hear with their **ears**. You have an **ear** on each side of your head. *Elephants have big ears.*

east

East is where the Sun comes up in the morning. The opposite direction is **west**.

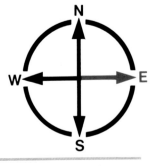

52

easy (easier, easiest)

If something is **easy** to do, it is simple and it can be done without working very hard. *This puzzle is very **easy**.*

eat (eating, ate, eaten)

When you **eat**, you put food in your mouth and it goes down into your stomach.

echo (echoes)

An **echo** is the sound that comes back to you when you shout in a place like a cave.

edge

An **edge** is the end or side of something. *Please don't put that glass so near the **edge** of the table.*

egg

Birds, fish, reptiles, and some other animals lay **eggs**. The young of these animals live inside **eggs** until they are ready to hatch. Hens lay **eggs** with hard shells that we use as food.

elbow

Your **elbows** are the parts in the middle of your arms where they bend.

electricity

Electricity is a kind of power that travels along wires. It makes heat and light, and it makes things like televisions and computers work.

elephant

An **elephant** is a very big, gray animal. Its long nose is called a trunk and it has two long teeth called tusks.

emerald

An **emerald** is a green jewel that is worth a lot of money.

empty (emptier, emptiest)

If something is **empty**, it has nothing or nobody inside. *This bottle is **empty**. Who drank all the orange juice?*

end

1 The **end** of something is the last part or the finish. *You hold one **end** of the ladder and I'll hold the other. I'm almost at the **end** of my book.*
2 (ending, ended) To **end** means to finish. *What time does this movie **end**?*

energy

Energy makes things move and engines work. Electricity is one kind of **energy**. You use your own **energy** when you run or jump.

engine

An **engine** is a machine that makes things like cars and airplanes move.

Wordplay
E is a very useful letter. An **e** at the end of a word changes the sound of the vowel (a, e, i, o, u) that comes earlier in the word.

not + e = note

What new words can you make by adding an **e** to the end of these words?

plan

hop   cub

kit   bar

e

Answers at the back!

---

enjoy (enjoying, enjoyed)

When you **enjoy** yourself, you feel happy about what you are doing. *Did you **enjoy** yourself at the birthday party?*

enormous

If something is **enormous**, it is very big. *An elephant is an **enormous** animal.*

enough

If you have **enough**, you have as much as you need or want. *Have you had **enough** to eat?*

enter (entering, entered)

When you **enter** a room or a building, you go in. *The man **entered** the store.*

envelope

An **envelope** is a thing made of paper that covers a letter when you send it. You stick stamps on an **envelope**.

environment

The **environment** is everything around us, like the air that we breathe and the water that we drink. *Some animals and plants will disappear forever if we don't do more to protect the **environment**.*

equal

1 If two things are **equal**, they are the same size or number. *We have **equal** numbers of apples and oranges.*
2 (equaling, equaled) If one thing **equals** another thing, they are the same size or the same number. *Two plus two **equals** four.*

escape (escaping, escaped)

When you **escape**, you get free or you get away from somebody or something. *My hamster has **escaped** from its cage.*

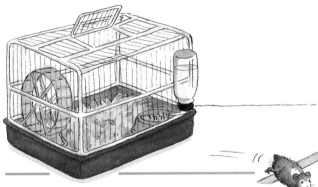

even

An **even** number is any number that ends in 2, 4, 6, 8, or 0. These numbers can be divided by 2 with nothing left over. The opposite of **even** is odd.

evening

The **evening** is the part of the day between afternoon and night. *The Sun goes down in the **evening**.*

ever

1 **Ever** means at any time. *Have you **ever** flown in an airplane?*
2 **Ever** also means for all time. *They lived happily **ever** after.*

evil

Evil means very, very bad. *In the story, the country was ruled by an **evil** king who treated his people very badly.*

excellent

Something that is **excellent** is very, very good. *We went to see an **excellent** movie last Saturday.*

except

Except means leaving out somebody or something. *All the puppies are brown **except** the little one, which is white.*

excited

If you are **excited**, you are so happy that you cannot keep quiet or stand still. *We're getting very **excited** about our vacation.*

excuse

An **excuse** is what you say to explain why you did or did not do something. *What is your **excuse** for being so late?*

exercise

1 Exercise is something, like running or jumping, that you do to keep your body strong and well. *We do lots of different exercises in the gym at school.*
2 An **exercise** is a small piece of work that you do to help you learn something. *Finish exercise 3 before you go out to play.*

exit

An **exit** is the way out of a building. *Can you show me where the exit is, please?*

expect (expecting, expected)

If you **expect** something, you think that it will happen. *I'm expecting my friend to phone today.*

expensive

Something that is **expensive** costs a lot of money to buy. *New bikes are very expensive.*

explain (explaining, explained)

When you **explain** something, you tell people about it so that they can understand. *Can you explain to me how this machine works?*

explode (exploding, exploded)

When something **explodes**, it breaks into pieces with a loud noise. *The fireworks exploded in the sky.*

explore (exploring, explored)

When you **explore**, you look carefully around a place you have never seen before.

On vacation, the children explored the woods to see what they could find.

extra

Extra means more than usual. *Emily asked for an extra slice of cake.*

eye

Your **eyes** are the parts of your face that you use for seeing.

Another word that sounds like **eye** is **I**.

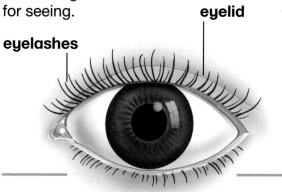

eyelashes

eyelid

Ff

face

Your **face** is the front part of your head. Your eyes, nose, and mouth are on your **face**.

fact

A **fact** is something that is true. *It is a fact that the world is round.*

factory (factories)

A **factory** is a building where people use machines to make things. *Cars are made in factories.*

fair

1 Something that is **fair** seems right. *You must be fair—if you give Emma a gift, you should give one to Elliot as well.*
2 Fair hair has a light color.
3 A **fair** is a place outside where you can have fun by riding on big machines with seats and playing games to win prizes. *I won a doll at a fair.*

fairy (fairies)

A **fairy** is a very small person that you can read about in stories. **Fairies** have magic powers and they can fly.

fall (falling, fell, fallen)

1 When somebody or something **falls**, it suddenly comes down to the ground. *She fell over on the playground.* **2 Fall** also means autumn.

false

If something is **false**, it is not true or not real. *The man gave a false name to the police instead of his real name.*

family (families)

A **family** is a group of people made up of parents, grandparents, and children. If you have aunts, uncles, and cousins, they are also part of your **family**.

famous

A **famous** person or thing is well known. *The Eiffel Tower is a famous tower in France.*

far (farther, farthest)

Far means a long way. *I can't walk to school—it's too **far**.*

farm

A **farm** is a place where people keep animals or grow crops for food. The person who looks after a **farm** is called a **farmer**.

farther Look at **far**.

fast

Something that is **fast** can move quickly. *I can run **faster** than my brother.*

fat

1 (fatter, fattest) A person or an animal that is **fat** has a big, round body. *Our dog is very **fat** because she eats a lot.*
2 Fat is also something like oil or butter that you can use in cooking.

father

A **father** is a man who has a child.

fault

If something bad is your **fault**, you made it happen. *It isn't my **fault** that we're late.*

favorite

Your **favorite** is the one that you like best. *What is your **favorite** color?*

fear

Fear is the feeling of being afraid. *Many animals have a **fear** of water.*

feather

Birds have **feathers** all over their bodies. **Feathers** are very light.

feed (feeding, fed)

If you **feed** an animal, you give food to it.

*We like **feeding** the ducks in the park.*

feel (feeling, felt)

1 When you **feel** something, you touch it to find out what it is like. ***Feel** this wool—it's really soft.*
2 When you **feel** sick, hot, or tired, you are that way at the moment. *I **felt** sad when my cat ran away.*

feet Look at **foot**.

fell Look at **fall**.

felt Look at **feel**.

female

A **female** person or animal belongs to the sex that can have babies.

Women and girls are **female**.

fence

A **fence** is a thing like a wall that is usually made of wood or wire. People put **fences** around yards, gardens, and fields.

ferry (ferries)

A **ferry** is a boat that carries cars and people. *We took a **ferry** to the island on our vacation.*

few

Few means not many. *We invited a lot of friends to the party, but only a **few** of them could come.*

field

A **field** is a piece of land where farmers grow crops or keep animals. Many **fields** have fences or stone walls around them.

fierce

An animal that is **fierce** is angry and dangerous. *Tigers can be **fierce**.*

fight (fighting, fought)

When people or animals **fight**, they try to hurt each other.

fill (filling, filled)

When you **fill** something, you put as much into it as you can.

*Dean is **filling** the glass with juice.*

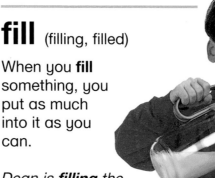

film

1 A **film** is a story in moving pictures that you watch on a screen.
2 A **film** is also a roll of thin plastic that you put in a camera for taking photographs.

find (finding, found)

When you **find** something, you see what you were looking for. *I lost my watch, but my friend **found** it on the playground.*

fine

Fine means very good. *I hope the weather stays **fine** for our picnic. I had a cold last week, but I feel **fine** now.*

finger

Your **fingers** are the five long, thin parts at the end of your hand.

finish (finishes, finishing, finished)

When you **finish** something, you come to the end of it. *When I've **finished** my painting, I'll show it to you.*

fire

Fire is the hot, bright light that comes from things that are burning.

fire fighter

A **fire fighter** is a person who has the job of putting out fires. A group of **fire fighters** who work together is called a **fire department**. They travel to fires in a big truck called a **fire engine**.

fireworks

Fireworks are things that send out showers of colored lights when somebody lights them. **Fireworks** often make a loud noise when they explode.

firm

Something that is **firm** is not soft or it does not move or change shape much when you touch it. *Bananas are **firm** when they are green, but they get softer when they are ripe.*

first

First means at the front or at the beginning. *I won the race—I came **first**. January is the **first** month of the year.*

fish (fish or fishes)

A **fish** is an animal that lives under water. A **fish** has fins and a tail to help it swim around. Its body is covered in lots of small parts called scales.

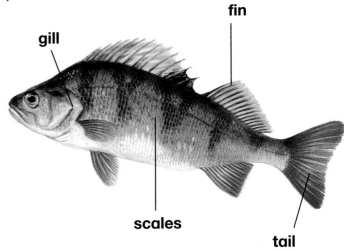

gill

fin

scales

tail

fist

A **fist** is a hand that is closed tightly. *John knocked on the door with his **fist**.*

fit

1 (fitting, fitted) If something **fits**, it is the right size and shape. *These shoes don't fit Rosa anymore. They're too small.*
2 (fitter, fittest) If you are **fit**, you are strong and healthy. *My dad does exercises to keep himself fit.*

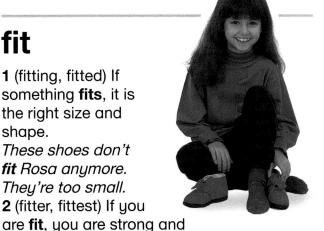

fix (fixing, fixed)

If you **fix** something that is broken, you make it useful again. *Katie is trying to fix my bike.*

flag

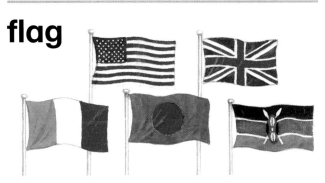

A **flag** is a piece of cloth with a colored pattern on it. **Flags** are hung on the end of a long pole. *Every country has its own flag.*

flame

A **flame** is a hot, bright light that you see when something is burning.

flap (flapping, flapped)

When a bird **flaps** its wings, it moves them quickly up and down.

flashlight

A **flashlight** is a small lamp that you can carry in your hand. *When we went camping we took a flashlight with us.*

flat (flatter, flattest)

Something that is **flat** is smooth and has no parts that are higher than the rest. *A table has a flat top. I need somewhere flat to do my puzzle.*

flavor

The **flavor** of food or drink is what it tastes like. *Which flavor ice cream do you like best—chocolate or strawberry?*

flew Look at **fly**.

Wordplay
How many words beginning with **f** can you make from these letters? You can use each letter as many times as you want.

Answers at the back!

61

Flowers

crocus

carnation

poppy

sunflower

petal

bud

stem

leaf

daffodil

tulip

lily

violet

rose

Flying seeds
Some flower **seeds** are carried by the wind.

flies Look at **fly**.

float
(floating, floated)

1 When something **floats** in a liquid, it stays on the top.
2 When something **floats** in air, it moves along gently in the air without falling. *I let go of the balloon and it **floated** away.*

flood

A **flood** happens when a lot of water covers a place that is usually dry. **Floods** usually happen when there has been a lot of rain.

floor

A **floor** is the flat part of a room that you walk on. *Some children had to sit on the **floor** because there were not enough chairs.*

flour

Flour is a white or brown powder that is made from wheat. We use **flour** to make bread and cakes.

Another word that sounds like **flour** is **flower**.

flow (flowing, flowed)

When a liquid **flows**, it moves along. *The river **flows** into the sea.*

flower

A **flower** is the pretty, colored part of a plant. *We gave Jenny some **flowers** on her birthday.*

Another word that sounds like **flower** is **flour**.

fly

1 (flies, flying, flew, flown) When a bird, an insect, or an aircraft **flies**, it moves through the air.
2 (flies) A **fly** is a small insect with wings.

foal

A **foal** is a young horse. *The **foal** was born last spring.*

fog

Fog is thick, cloudy air near the ground. *It is difficult to see through **fog**.*

fold (folding, folded)

If you **fold** something, you bend one part so that it covers another.

*Tom is **folding** up his clothes before he puts them away.*

follow (following, followed)

If you **follow** something or somebody, you go behind them. *The dog followed me along the street.*

food

Food is everything that people and animals eat. We eat **food** to stay alive and to grow.

foot (feet)

Your **foot** is the part at the end of your leg. You stand on your **feet**.

football

Football is a game for two teams who kick, run with, or throw a ball to score points.

foreign

A person or thing that is **foreign** comes from another country.

forest

A **forest** is a place where there are a lot of trees growing together. *A lot of different birds and animals live in the forest.*

forget (forgetting, forgot, forgotten)

When you **forget** something, you do not remember it. *I have forgotten where I put my book. Have you seen it? I forgot to send Ben a card on his birthday.*

fork

A **fork** is a tool with long pointed parts at one end. You use a small **fork** for putting food in your mouth. Big **forks** are used for digging the ground.

forward

Forward means toward what is in front. *The car started to move forward. The rope was swinging backward and forward.*

fossil

A **fossil** is a dead animal or plant that has turned to stone after it has been in the ground for a long time.

fought Look at **fight**.

found Look at **find**.

Some words, such as **phone**, sound as though they begin with **f**, but you will find them in the dictionary under **ph**.

fox

A **fox** is a wild animal with red-brown fur and a long, thick tail.

frame

A **frame** is the wooden or metal part around something like a picture or a window.

free

1 If something is **free**, you do not have to pay for it. *We got **free** tickets for the play because my dad works in the theater.*
2 If a person or an animal is **free**, they can go where they want and do what they want. *I opened the cage and set the bird **free**.*

freeze (freezing, froze, frozen)

1 When water **freezes**, it becomes ice.
2 If you are **freezing**, you are very cold. *Could you close the window, please? I'm **freezing**.*

fresh

1 Food that is **fresh** is not old or bad.
2 **Fresh** water is water that is not salty. *Rivers and most lakes have **fresh** water in them.*
3 **Fresh** air is air that is clean and good to breathe.

fridge

Fridge is a short and easy way to say the word **refrigerator**.

fried Look at **fry**.

friend

A **friend** is somebody you know well and like a lot. *Katie is my best **friend**.*

friendly (friendlier, friendliest)

A **friendly** person is kind and helpful.

frighten (frightening, frightened)

If you **frighten** somebody, you make them afraid. *My little brother is **frightened** of the dark.*

frog

A **frog** is a small animal that lives in and near water. **Frogs** have strong back legs that help them jump and swim.

front

The **front** of something is the part that you usually see first. *Harry's new book has a picture of two pandas on the **front**.*

frost

When there is a **frost**, the ground is covered with ice that looks like white powder.

frown (frowning, frowned)

When you **frown**, you make a face to show that you are sad, worried, angry, or that you are thinking hard.

froze Look at **freeze**.

frozen Look at **freeze**.

fruit

Fruit is a part of a plant that has the seeds in it. *Apples, oranges, and grapes are different kinds of fruit that we eat.*

fry (frying, fried)

If you **fry** food, you cook it in a pan in hot oil.

full

Something that is **full** has no space for anything else. *Charlotte's glass is full.*

fun

When you have **fun**, you enjoy yourself. *We all had a lot of fun at the birthday party.*

funny (funnier, funniest)

1 Something that is **funny** makes you laugh or smile. *My friend told me a funny joke.*
2 Funny also means strange. *The machine is making a funny noise.*

fur

Fur is the soft, thick hair that covers the skin of many animals. Cats, dogs, and bears are covered in **fur**.

furniture

Furniture is things like tables, chairs, and beds that people have in their homes.

furry (furrier, furriest)

Something that is **furry** is covered in fur. *A bear is a furry animal.*

future

The **future** is the time that has not happened yet. *In the future, people may go to the Moon on vacation.*

Fruit

pineapple

banana

apple

pear

△ Some fruits have seeds inside a **core.**

lime

orange

grapefruit

peach

plum

cherry

apricot

△ Some fruits have a **pit** in the middle. The **seed** is inside this pit.

grape

lemon

watermelon

△ Many fruits have lots of **seeds** in the juicy inside part called the **flesh.**

strawberry

Plant a tree
You can try growing your own fruit tree by planting some seeds or a pit.

raspberry

blackberry

a b c d e f g h i j k l m n o p q r s t u v w x y z

Gg

gallop (galloping, galloped)

When a horse **gallops**, it runs very fast. *The horse is galloping around the field.*

game

A **game** is a way of playing that has special rules. *Tennis and football are games that you play with a ball. Go Fish is a game that you play with cards.*

gap

A **gap** is a space between two things. *I have a gap where my tooth has fallen out.*

garage

1 A **garage** is a building where people keep cars.
2 A **garage** is also a place that sells gas or where people fix cars.

garden

A **garden** is a piece of land near a house, where people grow flowers or vegetables.

gas (gases)

1 A **gas** is something like air that does not have a shape. The air is made of different **gases** mixed together.
2 Gas is also a liquid made from oil that makes cars run.

gate

A **gate** is a kind of door in a wall or a fence. *Close the gate to the field so that the horse can't get out.*

gave Look at **give**.

geese Look at **goose**.

gentle

If you are **gentle**, you are quiet and kind and you do things carefully. *Be gentle with the baby.*

gerbil

A **gerbil** is a small, furry animal with long back legs. *Some people keep gerbils in cages as pets.*

Games

checkers

Parcheesi

dice

board

counter

dominoes

tick-tack-toe

card game

bowling

electronic game

jump rope

ghost

A **ghost** is the shape of a dead person that some people say they have seen. *Emma is dressed up as a **ghost**.*

giant

A **giant** is a very big person that you can read about in stories.

gift

A gift is something you give to someone. *We gave my sister some skis for a birthday **gift**.*

giggle (giggling, giggled)

If you **giggle**, you laugh in a silly way. *The funny story made us all **giggle**.*

giraffe

A **giraffe** is a very tall, wild animal that lives in Africa. It has long legs and a very long neck.

girl

A **girl** is a female child who will grow up to be a woman.

give
(giving, gave, given)

When you **give** something, you let another person have it. *Clara **gave** Richard a present for his birthday.*

glad

If you are **glad**, you are happy. *I'm **glad** you can come to my party.*

glass

1 Glass is a smooth, hard material that you can see through. *Windows and car windshields are made of **glass**.*
2 (glasses) A **glass** is a kind of cup made of glass. *May I have a **glass** of milk?*

glasses

People wear **glasses** over their eyes to help them see better. **Glasses** are made of a special kind of glass in a metal or plastic frame.

glove

People wear **gloves** to keep their hands warm or to protect them. **Gloves** have parts that cover each finger.

glue

Glue is a sticky liquid that you use to join things together.

goal

1 A **goal** is the place where you have to make the ball go to score a point in games like football or soccer.
2 A **goal** is also the point or points that you score when a ball goes into the **goal** area.

goat

A **goat** is an animal with rough hair. Some goats have horns. A young **goat** is called a kid.

gold

Gold is a shiny, yellow metal that people use to make jewelry, coins, and other things.

good (better, best)

1 When something is **good**, people like it. *That movie was really good.*
2 If you are **good**, you do as you are told.
3 If you are **good** at something, you can do it well. *Are you good at spelling?*
4 If something is **good** for you, it makes you healthy. *Eating fresh fruit is good for you.*

goose (geese)

A **goose** is a big bird with a long neck that swims well and lives near water. A young **goose** is called a gosling.

grab (grabbing, grabbed)

If you **grab** something, you take it quickly and roughly. *The robber grabbed the money and ran away.*

grade

A grade is one step in a row of things. *There are twelve grades in school.*

grandparent

Your **grandparents** are the mother and father of your mother or father. *My grandparents gave me some money for my birthday.*

grape

A **grape** is a small, round fruit that grows in bunches. **Grapes** are green or purple.

grapefruit

A **grapefruit** is a big, round, yellow fruit. **Grapefruits** are like oranges, but they are not as sweet.

Grapefruits got their name because they grow in bunches, like huge grapes.

Wordplay
This ghost message is disappearing! Can you read it?

Well done

Answer at the back!

grass (grasses)

Grass is a plant with thin, green leaves that covers fields, parks, and lawns. *Horses and cows eat grass.*

great

1 Great means very good. *We had a great time at the beach.*
2 Great also means very important and famous. *The king was a great leader.*
3 Great also means very big. *There was a great crowd of people outside the theater.*

greedy (greedier, greediest)

A person who is **greedy** wants more of something than they really need. *Don't be greedy—leave some cake for your brother.*

grew Look at grow.

ground

The **ground** is what you walk on when you are outside. *A bird landed on the ground near my feet.*

group

A **group** is a number of people or things that are together in one place. *A group of children stood outside the school.*

grow (growing, grew, grown)

When something **grows**, it gets bigger and bigger. *Animals and plants grow.*

grown-up

A **grown-up** is a person who has finished growing. *Parents are grown-ups.*

guard (guarding, guarded)

To **guard** means to watch somebody or something all the time to make sure that nothing bad happens. *Our neighbors have a big dog to guard their house.*

guess (guesses, guessing, guessed)

When you **guess**, you try to give the answer to something without really knowing if it is right. *Can you guess how many apples are in my bag?*

guitar

A **guitar** is a musical instrument with strings that you play with your fingers.

gym

A **gym** is a room where people play games and do exercises. *Our school has a big gym.*

habit

A **habit** is something that you do often. *Biting your nails is a bad **habit**.*

hair

Hair is what grows on your head. Animals and people have **hair**.

half (halves)

A **half** is one of two pieces of something that are the same size. *I had one **half** of the orange and my friend had the other **half**.*

hall

A **hall** is the space inside a building that has doors leading to other rooms.

Halloween

Halloween is October 31. *Some people believe that witches and ghosts appear at **Halloween**.*

halves Look at **half**.

hamburger

A **hamburger** is a round, flat piece of ground beef in a bun.

hammer

A **hammer** is a heavy tool that people use for hitting nails into wood or walls.

hamster

A **hamster** is a small, furry animal. They have large cheeks where they can store food. *Some people keep **hamsters** as pets.*

hand

Your **hands** are the parts of your body at the ends of your arms. A **hand** has four fingers and a thumb. *We use our **hands** for picking things up and holding them.*

a b c d e f g **h** i j k l m n o p q r s t u v w x y z

handle

A **handle** is the part of something that you use to carry or hold it. Things like doors, cups, and scissors have **handles**.

hang (hanging, hung)

Something that is **hanging** is joined at the top to something above it. *The clothes are hanging out to dry.*

happy (happier, happiest)

If you are **happy**, you feel good about something. You smile when you are **happy**.

hard

1 If something is **hard**, you cannot break or cut it easily, or shape it with your hands. *Stone is hard.*
2 Something that is **hard** is difficult. *I can't do this puzzle. It's too hard.*

hat

A **hat** is something you wear on your head.

hatch (hatches, hatching, hatched)

When a baby bird **hatches**, it breaks out of its egg. *Three chicks hatched this morning.*

hate (hating, hated)

If you **hate** something, you have a very strong feeling of not liking it.

hay

Hay is dry grass that is used for feeding animals.

head

1 Your **head** is the top part of your body that has your eyes, ears, and mouth in it.
2 The **head** is also the leader. *What's the name of the head of the school band?*

heal (healing, healed)

When something like a cut **heals**, it gets well again. *His broken leg healed quickly.*

healthy (healthier, healthiest)

If you are **healthy**, you are not sick.

hear (hearing, heard)

When you **hear** sounds, you notice them with your ears.

Another word that sounds like **hear** is **here**.

heart

Your **heart** is inside your chest. It sends blood to all parts of your body.

heat

1 (heating, heated) If you **heat** something, you make it hot. *David **heated** some milk in a saucepan.*
2 Heat also means being warm or hot. *Stand by the fire—the **heat** will dry your wet clothes quickly.*

heavy (heavier, heaviest)

Something that is **heavy** is difficult to lift or move. *These books are too **heavy** for Tom to pick up.*

hedge

A **hedge** is a line of bushes or small trees that make a kind of wall.

heel

1 Your **heel** is the back part of your foot.
2 A **heel** is also the back part of a shoe.

height

The **height** of something or somebody is how tall they are.

*What **height** are you?*

held Look at **hold**.

helicopter

A **helicopter** is an aircraft without wings. It has long sharp parts, called rotors, which turn around on top.

helmet

A **helmet** is a hard hat that people wear to protect their heads. *Gemmel is wearing a bicycle **helmet**.*

help (helping, helped)

If you **help** somebody, you do something useful for them. *I **helped** my teacher by carrying the books for her.*

hen

A **hen** is a female chicken. **Hens** lay eggs.

hide (hiding, hid, hidden)

1 When you **hide**, you go into a place where people cannot see you.

*Harry is **hiding** from his friends.*

2 When you **hide** something, you put it where people cannot see it. *I **hid** my sister's shoes under the bed.*

high

Something that is **high** goes up a long way. *This wall is very **high**. Mount Everest is the **highest** mountain in the world.*

hill

A **hill** is a piece of ground that is higher than the land around it. *We climbed to the top of the **hill**.*

hippo

A **hippo** is a big, wild animal that lives in and near rivers and lakes in hot countries. **Hippo** is short for **hippopotamus**.

Hippopotamus is made from two Greek words that mean "river horse."

Wordplay
Play this dictionary game with a friend. Open the dictionary at any page and read out the first and last words on that page. Your friend must try to guess any of the other words on the page!

hit (hitting, hit)

If you **hit** somebody or something, you touch it very hard. *I tried to **hit** the ball with the bat.*

hobby (hobbies)

A **hobby** is something that you enjoy doing when you have free time. *My **hobbies** are swimming, reading, and collecting stamps.*

hockey

Hockey is a game played on ice. Each team tries to get a disk called a puck into a goal.

hold
(holding, held)

1 When you **hold** something, you have it in your hand. *Bobby is **holding** a bunch of flowers.*

2 Hold also means to have something inside. *This bottle **holds** a quart of water.*

hole

A **hole** is an empty space or gap. *Joe has a **hole** in his sock.*

Another word that sounds like **hole** is **whole**.

holiday (holidays)

A **holiday** is a special time when you do not go to work or school. *What did you do over the Thanksgiving **holiday**?*

hollow

Something that is **hollow** has an empty space inside. *A drum is **hollow**.*

home

Your **home** is the place where you live.

honest *say onnist

If somebody is **honest**, they always tell the truth. *If you are **honest**, people will trust you.*

honey

Honey is a thick, sweet food that bees make.

hop (hopping, hopped)

1 When you **hop**, you jump on one foot.
2 When an animal **hops**, it moves in small jumps. *Rabbits, frogs, and some other animals **hop**.*

hope (hoping, hoped)

If you **hope** that something will happen, you want it to happen and you think that it might. *I **hope** you will be able to come to my party.*

horn

A **horn** is a hard, pointed thing that grows out of the heads of some animals, like goats, bulls, and some sheep.

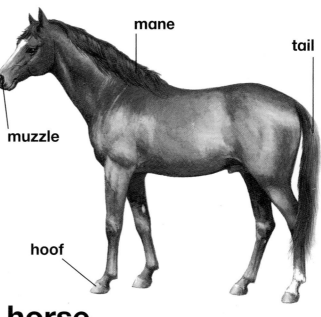

mane

tail

muzzle

hoof

horse

A **horse** is an animal with a long tail and long hair, called a mane, on its neck. People ride **horses** and use them for pulling things like wagons. A young **horse** is called a foal.

hospital

A **hospital** is a large building where doctors and nurses look after people who are sick. *We went to visit my aunt in the **hospital**.*

The human body

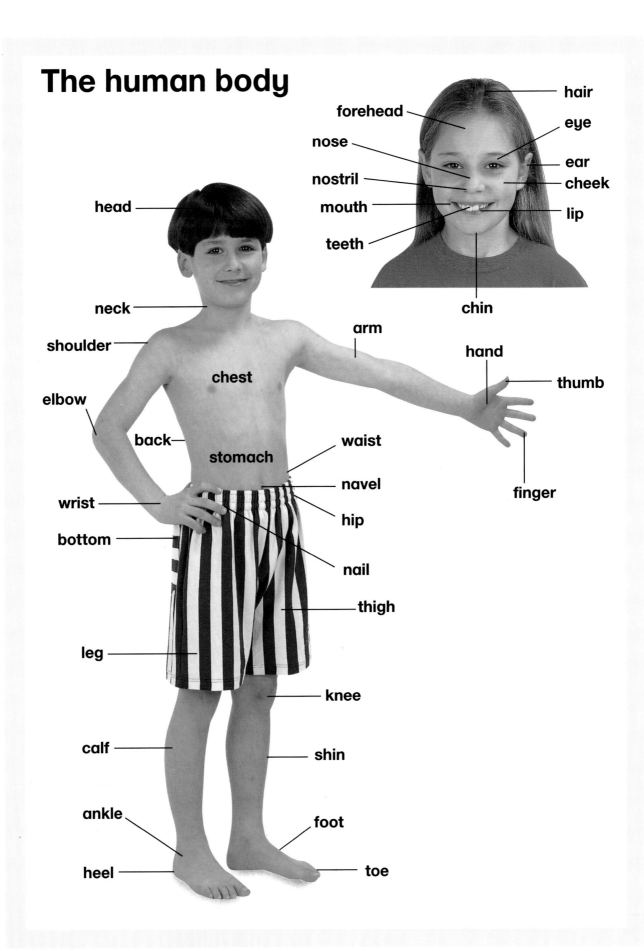

hair
forehead
eye
nose
ear
nostril
cheek
mouth
lip
teeth
head
chin
neck
arm
hand
shoulder
thumb
chest
elbow
back
finger
waist
stomach
navel
wrist
hip
bottom
nail
thigh
leg
knee
calf
shin
ankle
foot
heel
toe

a b c d e f g h i j k l m n o p q r s t u v w x y z

hot (hotter, hottest)

The Sun is **hot**, and so is fire. **Hot** things can burn you. *An oven gets very hot inside.*

hotel

A **hotel** is a building with a lot of bedrooms, where people can stay when they are away from home.

hour

An **hour** is a time of 60 minutes. There are 24 **hours** in a day.

Another word that sounds like **hour** is **our**.

house

A **house** is a building where people live. *How many rooms does your house have?*

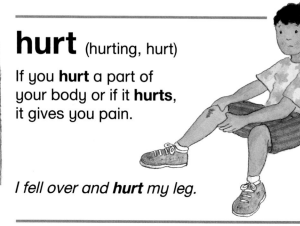

huge

If something is **huge**, it is very big.

human

A **human** is a person.

hump

A **hump** is a big round part on an animal's back. Camels have one or two **humps**.

hung Look at **hang**.

hungry (hungrier, hungriest)

When you are **hungry**, you feel that you want to eat something.

hunt (hunting, hunted)

1 When animals **hunt**, they chase other animals and kill them for food.
2 When you **hunt** for something, you look carefully for it. *I hunted all over the house for my book.*

hurry (hurries, hurrying, hurried)

When you **hurry**, you go somewhere or do something as quickly as you can. *If you don't hurry, you will be late for school.*

hurt (hurting, hurt)

If you **hurt** a part of your body or if it **hurts**, it gives you pain.

I fell over and hurt my leg.

husband

A woman's **husband** is the man she is married to.

hut

A **hut** is a small, simple building. **Huts** usually have only one room inside. *Many huts are made of wood or grass.*

79

ice

Ice is water that has become hard because it is very cold.

ice cream

Ice cream is a sweet, frozen food.

icicle

An **icicle** is a long piece of ice hanging down from something.

idea

When you have an **idea**, you think of something. *Do you have any good ideas for games we can play at the party?*

igloo

An **igloo** is a house made of blocks of snow or ice.

ill

When you are **ill**, you are not well. *My sister is staying in bed today because she's ill.*

imagine (imagining, imagined)

When you **imagine** something, you have a picture of it in your mind. *Close your eyes and imagine you are on the beach.*

immediately

If you do something **immediately**, you do it now, without waiting. *We must leave immediately or we'll miss our train.*

important

1 Something that is **important** matters a lot. *It is important to look both ways before you cross the road.*
2 If somebody is **important,** they have a lot of power. *The president of the United States is a very important person.*

impossible

If you say something is **impossible**, it cannot be done. *It's impossible for a person to walk on the ceiling.*

information

Information is the facts about something. *This dictionary gives you information about words and how to spell them.*

ink

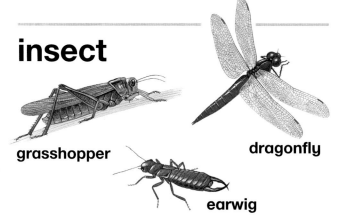

Ink is the colored liquid that is used for writing or printing. *The words on this page were printed with **ink**.*

insect

grasshopper

dragonfly

earwig

An **insect** is a very small creature with six legs. Many **insects** have wings. Earwigs, grasshoppers, and dragonflies are **insects**.

inside

If you are **inside** something, it is all around you. *The fish is swimming around **inside** its bowl.*

instead

Instead means in the place of something. *I don't like tea—can I have water **instead**?*

instrument

1 An **instrument** is something that is used for doing a special job. *A telescope is an **instrument** that is used for looking at things that are far away.*
2 A musical **instrument** is something that you play to make music. *Guitars and pianos are musical **instruments**.*

interesting

If something is **interesting**, you like it and want to find out more about it. *Our school visit to the museum was very **interesting**.*

invent (inventing, invented)

If you **invent** something, you make something that has never been made or thought of before. *Thomas Edison was a famous **inventor**. He **invented** the light bulb.*

invisible

If something is **invisible**, it cannot be seen.

invite (inviting, invited)

If you **invite** somebody, you ask them to come somewhere to do something. *My brother has **invited** ten friends to his birthday party. He has sent them all **invitations**.*

iron

1 Iron is a strong, hard metal.
2 An **iron** is a tool that we use to make clothes smooth. **Irons** are flat on the bottom and they get very hot.

island *say eyeland

An **island** is a piece of land with water all around it.

jacket

A **jacket** is a short coat.

jam

1 Jam is a sweet food made by cooking fruit with sugar.
2 (jamming, jammed) If something **jams**, it becomes difficult to move. *The window won't open—it's **jammed**.*

jar

A **jar** is a wide glass bottle. Jam and a lot of other foods come in **jars**.

jaw

Your **jaw** is the bone at the bottom of your face. You move your **jaw** when you eat and speak.

jeans

Jeans are pants that are made of strong cotton cloth called denim.

jelly (jellies)

Jelly is a sweet food made with fruit and sugar.

jet

A **jet** is an aircraft that can fly very fast.

jewel

A **jewel** is a beautiful stone that is worth a lot of money. Diamonds, emeralds, and rubies are **jewels**.

job

1 A **job** is something that you have to do. *It's my brother's **job** to wash the dishes after dinner.*
2 Somebody's **job** is the work that they do to get money.

jog (jogging, jogged)

To **jog** means to run slowly. *My mom **jogs** around the park every morning.*

Some words such as **gentle**, sound as though they begin with **j**, but you will find them in the dictionary under **g**.

join (joining, joined)

1 If you **join** a group, you become part of it. *I've **joined** a football team.*
2 If you **join** things, you put or stick them together.

joke

A **joke** is something that you say or do to make people laugh.

joy

Joy is a feeling of being very happy. *Everybody jumped for **joy** at the sight of all the cake and ice cream at the birthday party.*

juice

Juice is the liquid that comes from fruit. *Would you like orange **juice** or grapefruit **juice** to drink?*

jump (jumping, jumped)

When you **jump**, you move suddenly into the air.

jumper

A **jumper** is a sleeveless dress that you wear over a shirt. *Each girl in the chorus wore a green **jumper** with a shirt underneath.*

jungle

A **jungle** is a thick forest in a hot country.

junk

Junk is things that are old and not useful anymore. *This box is full of **junk**.*

Wordplay
How many clothes words can you find by reading across and down in this word search box? Look at page 34 if you need any help.

x	i	s	p	d	e
f	b	c	a	p	s
j	e	a	n	s	o
u	l	r	t	h	c
p	t	f	s	o	k
g	l	o	v	e	t

Answers at the back!

Kk

kangaroo
(kangaroos)

A **kangaroo** is a wild animal that lives in Australia. It has strong back legs and moves by making long jumps.

A female **kangaroo** has a sort of bag at the front of her body where she keeps her baby.

keep (keeping, kept)

1 If you **keep** something, you hold onto it and do not give it away. *You can keep this book—I don't need it.*
2 When you **keep** something in a place, you have it there. *You must keep your money somewhere safe.*
3 If you **keep** doing something, you do it many times. *My little brother keeps following me around.*
4 Keep also means to stay in the same way. *Keep still while I take your photo.*

kept Look at **keep**.

ketchup

Ketchup is a kind of food made from tomatoes. *I would like lots of ketchup on my hamburger.*

kettle

A **kettle** is a pot with a lid, a handle, and a pointed part, called a spout, for pouring. You use a **kettle** for heating water.

key
(keys)

1 A **key** is a piece of metal that you turn to lock or unlock something.
2 The **keys** of a piano or a computer are the parts that you press with your fingers.

kick (kicking, kicked)

If you **kick** something, you hit it with your foot.

Harry has kicked the ball.

kid

1 A **kid** is a young goat.
2 People also sometimes call children **kids.**

kill (killing, killed)

To **kill** means to make somebody or something die.

kind

1 A **kind** person is nice to other people and ready to help them.
2 A **kind** is a group of things that are the same in some way. *Kangaroos and elephants are two **kinds** of animal.*

king

Some countries are ruled by a man called a **king**. The wife of a **king** is called a queen.

kingdom

A **kingdom** is a country that is ruled by a king or queen. *The king was the richest man in the whole **kingdom**.*

kiss (kisses, kissing, kissed)

When you **kiss** somebody, you touch them with your lips in a friendly way.

kit

A **kit** is a set of things. *The driver took out her tool **kit** to fix the engine.*

kitchen

A **kitchen** is a room where food is cooked.

kite

A **kite** is a toy on the end of a long piece of string that you fly in the wind. **Kites** are made of paper, cloth, or plastic.

kitten

A **kitten** is a very young cat. *Our cat has just had **kittens**.*

knee *say *nee*

Your **knees** are the parts of your legs in the middle that bend.

kneel *say *neel*
(kneeling, knelt)

When you **kneel**, you go down on your knees.

knew Look at **know**.

Another word that sounds like **knew** is **new**.

knife *say *nife* (knives)

A **knife** is a tool for cutting. It has a handle and a long, sharp piece of metal called a blade.

knight *say *nite*

Long ago, a **knight** was a soldier who fought to protect a king or a queen.

Knights rode horses and many **knights** wore armor.

Another word that sounds like **knight** is **night**.

Wordplay
Put the words in each group in the order in which they come in the dictionary. If the first letter is the same, look at the second letter, and so on.

1 key, car, wheel

2 puppy, powder, pretty

3 triangle, true, tractor

Answers at the back!

---

knit *say *nit* (knitting, knitted)

When you **knit**, you use two long needles and wool to make clothes.

knock *say *nok* (knocking, knocked)

If you **knock** something, you hit it hard. *Nadia **knocked** on the door.*

knot *say *not*

You make a **knot** when you twist and tie pieces of string or thread together.

Another word that sounds like **knot** is **not**.

know *say *no* (knowing, knew, known)

1 If you **know** somebody, you have met them before. *I **know** her because she is in my class.*
2 If you **know** something, you have it in your mind. *Everybody **knows** their own name.*

Another word that sounds like **know** is **no**.

koala

A **koala** is an animal that looks like a small bear with thick, gray fur. It lives in trees and it is only found in Australia.

Ll

label

A **label** is a small note stuck to something. It may tell you what the thing is made of or who it belongs to.

lace

1 A **lace** is a thin string that you use to hold things together. *Tie your **shoelaces**.*
2 **Lace** is pretty cloth with a pattern of holes in it. *The dress had a collar made of **lace**.*

ladder

A **ladder** is a set of steps that you use for climbing up to a high place.

ladybug

A **ladybug** is a small, round beetle that can fly. **Ladybugs** are usually red with black spots.

laid

Look at **lay**.

lain

Look at **lie**.

lake

A **lake** is a lot of water with land all around it.

lamb

A **lamb** is a young sheep.

lamp

A **lamp** is something that gives out light in the dark. *I have a reading **lamp** by my bed.*

land

1 **Land** is the part of the Earth that is not covered in water.
2 (landing, landed) When something **lands**, it comes down from the air onto the ground. *The airplane **landed** in a field.*

language

Language is the words we use to speak, read, and write to each other. There are many different **languages** in the world, such as English, French, and Swahili.

lap

Your **lap** is the top of your legs when you are sitting down.
My cat likes to sit on my lap.

large

Something that is **large** is big. *Whales are very large animals.*

last

1 When somebody or something is **last**, it is at the end or after all the others. *Z is the last letter of the alphabet.*
2 Last also means the one before this one. *I went to bed late last night.*

late

If you are **late**, you get to a place after the time you were supposed to. *Sandra is often late for school.*

laugh (laughing, laughed)

When you **laugh**, you make sounds that show that you think something is funny.

law

A **law** is a rule of a country that everybody must keep. *Stealing is against the law.*

lawn

A **lawn** is the area covered with short grass around a house or another building.

lay (laying, laid)

1 When you **lay** something somewhere, you put it down carefully. *Sam laid the sheet of paper on the teacher's desk.*
2 To **lay** also means to make an egg. *Hens lay eggs.*
3 Look at **lie**.

layer

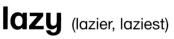

A **layer** is something flat that lies under or over something else. *The cake has a layer of frosting in the middle.*

lazy (lazier, laziest)

Somebody who is **lazy** does not want to do work or do very much. *I did not clean my room because I was feeling very lazy.*

lead *rhymes with *seed* (leading, led)

When you **lead** somebody, you go in front to show them where to go.

lead
*rhymes with *bed*

Lead is a very heavy, gray metal.

Another word that sounds like **lead** is **led**.

leader

A **leader** is the person who shows other people the way or who goes first.

leaf (leaves)

A **leaf** is one of the thin, flat parts that grow on plants.

Most **leaves** are green.

lean
(leaning, leaned)

To **lean** means to rest against something or to bend in one direction.
Paul is leaning against a tree.

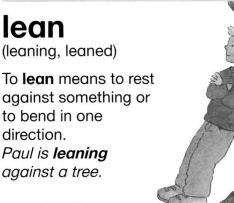

learn (learning, learned)

When you **learn** something, you find out about it or how to do it. *My little sister is learning to swim.*

leather

Leather is the skin of an animal. It is used to make things like shoes and gloves.

leave (leaving, left)

1 If you **leave**, you go away from a place. *What time do you leave home to go to school in the morning?*
2 If you **leave** something somewhere, it stays where it is. *Andrew left his bag at school so he had to go back to get it.*

leaves Look at **leaf**.

led Look at **lead**.

left

1 Left is the opposite of right. *Rosa has a puppet on her left hand.*
2 Look at **leave**.

leg

1 Legs are the long parts of a person's or an animal's body that are used for walking. *People have two legs.*
2 The **legs** of a chair or a table are the parts that it stands on.

lemon

A **lemon** is a yellow fruit with a sour taste.

length

The **length** of something is how long it is. *The children are measuring the length of the table.*

lesson

A **lesson** is a time when you learn something. *I have a piano **lesson** every Tuesday afternoon.*

letter

1 A **letter** is a message that you write on paper to another person.

*Amy's friend has sent her a **letter**.*

2 A **letter** is also one of the signs that we use for writing words. There are 26 **letters** in the English alphabet. *D, H, and Q are **letters**.*

lettuce

Lettuce is a plant with large green leaves that you can eat in salads.

library (libraries)

A **library** is a place where information is kept. People can borrow books, records, and many other things from a **library**.

lick (licking, licked)

When you **lick** something, you move your tongue over it.

lid

A **lid** is the top part of a box, jar, or other container. You lift the **lid** to open the container.

lie

1 A **lie** is something you say that you know is not true. *Our teacher told us that we should never tell **lies**.*
2 (lying, lay, lain) When you **lie** somewhere, you rest your body flat on something. *Paulo is **lying** on the floor reading a book.*

life (lives)

Life is the time when you are alive. *I shall remember that day for the rest of my **life**.*

lift

1 (lifting, lifted) If you **lift** something, you move it up.

*Dean can barely **lift** the box of toys.*

2 When talking about bad weather, **lift** also means to clear up or disappear. *The fog **lifted** when the Sun rose.*
3 If you get a **lift** with somebody, you travel with them in their car. *My neighbor gave me a **lift** to school this morning.*

light

1 **Light** is what comes from the Sun and from lamps. Without **light** you could not see anything.
2 Something that is **light** is not difficult to lift. *A bag feels very **light** when there is nothing inside it.*
3 Colors that are **light** are not very bright. *I have a **light** blue dress.*
4 (lighting, lit) When you **light** something, you make it burn. *Jenny's dad **lit** the candles on the cake.*

lighthouse

A **lighthouse** is a tower with a strong light on top that helps ships to see dangerous rocks when it is dark.

lightning

Lightning is a flash of light that you see in the sky when there is a thunderstorm.

like

1 When something is **like** something else, it is the same in some way. *Carla is wearing a dress **like** mine.*
2 (liking, liked) If you **like** something, it makes you happy. *I **like** dancing and reading books.*

likely

If something is **likely**, it will probably happen. *It's very cold, so it's **likely** to snow tonight.*

line

1 A **line** is a long, thin mark. *You can use a ruler to draw straight **lines** on paper.*

2 A **line** is also a row of people or things. *Our teacher asked us to stand in a **line**.*

lion

A **lion** is a large, wild cat. A female **lion** is called a lioness and a young **lion** is called a cub.

lip

Your **lips** are the soft, pink edges of your mouth.

liquid

A **liquid** is anything that is wet and that you can pour like water. *Orange juice, milk, and oil are all **liquids**.*

list

A **list** is a group of words or names that are written down one after the other. *We made a list so we could remember what to buy when we went shopping.*

shopping list
apples
milk
bread
cheese
vegetables
fish
stamps

listen (listening, listened)

When you **listen**, you carefully try to hear something. *Please listen to what I am saying. Do you ever listen to the radio?*

lit Look at **light**.

little

1 Something that is **little** is small in size. *The last toe on your foot is called your little toe.*
2 A **little** means not very much. *There is only a little juice left in Thomas's glass.*

Wordplay
Can you find a word on this page that makes a different word if you spell it backwards?

Try to think of other words that do this. Here are some clues.

Answers at the back!

live (living, lived)

1 To **live** means to be alive. *Dinosaurs lived millions of years ago.*
2 If you **live** somewhere, you have your home there. *My aunt and uncle live on a farm in New Mexico.*

lives Look at **life**.

loaf (loaves)

A **loaf** is bread in a shape that can be cut into slices.

lock

1 A **lock** is something that is used to keep things like doors and drawers shut, so that you cannot open them without a key.
2 (locking, locked) When you **lock** something, you close it with a key. *We locked all the doors and windows when we went out.*

log

A **log** is a large, round piece of wood that has been cut from a tree.

long

Something that is **long** measures a lot from one end to the other.

The monkey has a long tail.

look (looking, looked)

1 If you **look** at somebody or something, you turn your eyes so that you can see it. **Look** at this picture.

2 If you **look** for something, you try to find it. I'm **looking** for my book.

loose

If something is **loose**, it is not firmly stuck in one place. One of my teeth is **loose**.

lose (losing, lost)

1 When you **lose** something, you cannot find it. Mark has **lost** his glasses.

2 If you **lose** a game, you do not win it. Our team **lost** the match.

lost

If you are **lost**, you cannot find your way. Take this map so that you don't get **lost**.

lot

If you have a lot of something, you have very much of it. He ate a **lot** of cookies.

loud

Something that is **loud** makes a lot of noise. The music is too **loud**. Please turn it down.

love (loving, loved)

If you **love** something or somebody, you like them very, very much. I **love** ice cream.

lovely

Something that is **lovely** is beautiful or very nice. We had a **lovely** vacation.

low

Something that is **low** is not high. The fence was so **low** that Josie could step over it.

luggage

Luggage is all the bags that you carry your clothes in when you travel.

lumber

Lumber is wood that is used for building things.

lunch

Lunch is a meal that people eat in the middle of the day.

Dean is eating his **lunch**.

lying Look at lie.

Mm

machine

A **machine** is a thing with parts that move to do work or to make something. *Computers and cars are both machines.*

mad

If you are **mad**, you are very angry. *I got very mad at my best friend when he broke my bicycle.*

magic

Magic is a special power that is supposed to make strange and impossible things happen.

magician

A **magician** is a person who seems to make things happen by magic.

magnet

A **magnet** is a piece of metal that can pull other metal things toward it.

magnifying glass

A **magnifying glass** is a special piece of glass. When you look through it, things look bigger than they really are.

mail

The **mail** is the letters and packages sent and delivered. *Has the mail come yet?*

male

A **male** person or animal belongs to the sex that cannot have babies.

Boys and men are **male**.

mammal

A **mammal** is an animal that drinks milk from its mother's body when it is young. *People, horses, and whales are mammals.*

man (men)

A **man** is a grown-up male person.

map

A **map** is a drawing that shows you what a place looks like from above. **Maps** show things like roads and rivers, and they help you to find your way around a place.

marble

1 Marble is a kind of very hard stone that is used to make things like statues and buildings.

2 A **marble** is a small glass ball that is used in games.

march (marching, marched)

When people **march**, they walk together in straight lines and take steps at the same time.

mark

A **mark** is a spot or a line on something that spoils it.

marry (marries, marrying, married)

When two people **marry**, they agree to share their lives as husband and wife.

mask

A **mask** is something that you can wear over your face to hide it or to protect it.

match

1 (matches) A **match** is a small, thin stick that makes fire when you rub it on something rough.

2 (matches) A **match** is also a game between two teams or players. *We watched a tennis **match** on television.*

3 (matches, matching, matched) If one thing **matches** another, it has the same color, shape, or pattern.

*Katie's hat **matches** her scarf.*

material

1 A **material** is anything that is used to make other things. *Stone, wood, and glass are **materials** that we use to build houses.*

2 Material is cloth that we use to make clothes.

matter (mattering, mattered)

If something **matters**, it is important. *Ben has lost my ruler, but it doesn't **matter** because I have another one.*

mattress (mattresses)

A **mattress** is the soft, thick part of a bed.

meal

When you have a **meal**, you sit down and eat something.

Breakfast, lunch, and dinner are **meals**.

mean

1 (meaning, meant) If you ask what something **means**, you want somebody to explain it. *What does this word **mean**?*
2 (meaning, meant) If you **mean** to do something, you plan it and want to do it. *I didn't **mean** to step on your foot.*
3 Somebody who is **mean** is not very nice or does not like sharing.

measure

(measuring, measured)

When you **measure** something, you find out how big it is.

*David is **measuring** his workbook.*

meat

Meat is part of an animal that we use as food. *Beef is **meat** from a cow.*

Another word that sounds like **meat** is **meet**.

medicine

Medicine is something that you take when you are sick to make you feel better.

meet (meeting, met)

When you **meet** somebody, you go to the same place at the same time as them. ***Meet** me outside school at four o'clock.*

Another word that sounds like **meet** is **meat**.

melt (melting, melted)

When something **melts**, it changes into a liquid. *The snowman **melted** in the warm sun.*

memory

Memory is being able to remember things. If you have a good **memory**, you can remember lots of things.

men Look at **man**.

mend (mending, mended)

When you **mend** something that is broken, you make it useful again. *I have broken my kite—can you **mend** it?*

mention (mentioning, mentioned)

If you **mention** something, you say a little bit about it. *Did Jo **mention** her party?*

mess

A **mess** is when a lot of things are not where they belong. *Your bedroom is in a terrible mess—please clean it up!*

message

A **message** is words that you send to somebody or that you ask another person to pass on to them. *Tom isn't home. Would you like to leave a message for him?*

met Look at **meet**.

metal

Metal is a hard material that is used for making things like cars and airplanes. Silver and iron are different kinds of **metal**.

mice Look at **mouse**.

microscope

A **microscope** is an instrument that makes very small things look much bigger. *We looked at a drop of pond water under the microscope.*

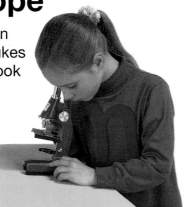

middle

The **middle** of something is the part that is not near the outside edges. *There is a vase of flowers in the middle of the table.*

midnight

Midnight is 12 o'clock at night.

milk

Milk is the white liquid that mothers make in their bodies to feed their babies. *People drink the milk that cows make.*

mind

1 Your **mind** is the part of you that you use for thinking and remembering.
2 If you do not **mind** something, you do not feel unhappy or angry about it. *I don't mind if you play with my toys.*
3 To **mind** also means to obey someone or something. *Mind your parents.*

mine

A **mine** is a place where people dig deep holes to find things like coal and gold.

minus

You use **minus** to talk about taking one number away from another. *Four minus one is three.*

minute *say min**nit**

A **minute** is a short time. There are 60 **minutes** in an hour.

mirror

A **mirror** is a piece of special glass that you can see yourself in.

miss (missing, missed)

1 If you **miss** something that you were trying to hit or catch, you do not hit or catch it. *I tried to hit the ball but I **missed** it.*
2 If you **miss** somebody, you are sad because you are not with them. *I'll **miss** you when you go away.*

mistake

A **mistake** is something you do that is wrong. *You have made some spelling **mistakes** in this letter.*

mix (mixing, mixed)

When you **mix** things, you stir them or put them together in some other way so that they make something new.

*If you **mix** blue and red paint, you get purple.*

model

A **model** is a small copy of something. *Sue is building a **model** of a sailboat.*

moment

A **moment** is a very short time. *Please wait for me—I will be ready in a **moment**.*

money

Money is the coins and special pieces of paper, called bills, that we use to pay for things.

monkey (monkeys)

A **monkey** is an animal with long arms and legs and a long tail. **Monkeys** live in hot countries. They are good at climbing and swinging from trees.

monster

A **monster** is a big, frightening creature that you can read about in stories.

month

A **month** is one of the 12 parts of a year. *January is the first **month** of the year.*

Moon

The **Moon** is an object in space that travels around the Earth once every four weeks. You can often see it in the sky at night.

morning

The **morning** is the early part of the day, before 12 o'clock.

moth

A **moth** is an insect with big wings. **Moths** look like butterflies, but they usually fly around at night.

mother

A **mother** is a woman who has a child.

motor

A **motor** is a machine that makes things move.

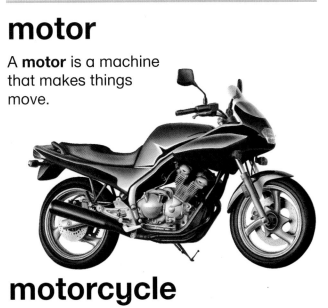

motorcycle

A **motorcycle** is a kind of big, heavy bicycle with an engine. *When my sister grows up she wants to buy a **motorcycle**.*

mountain

A **mountain** is a very high hill. *The highest mountain in the world is Mount Everest.*

mouse (mice)

A **mouse** is a small, furry animal with a long tail and sharp teeth.

mouth

Your **mouth** is the part of your face that you open and close to talk and eat.

Wordplay

Can you read this?

What are keys are furry? Monkeys!

Answer at the back!

Now try writing your own name so you can read it in a mirror.

abcdefghijklmnopqrstuvwxyz

Musical instruments

▽ You blow into the **mouthpiece** and press the **buttons** to play a **trumpet**.

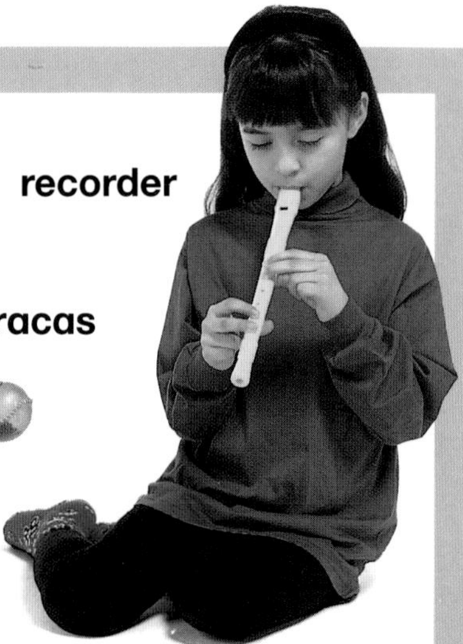

recorder

maracas

drum

▷ You move the **bow** across the **strings** of the **violin** to play it.

xylophone

cymbals

▽ A **piano** has **keys** that you press to make sounds.

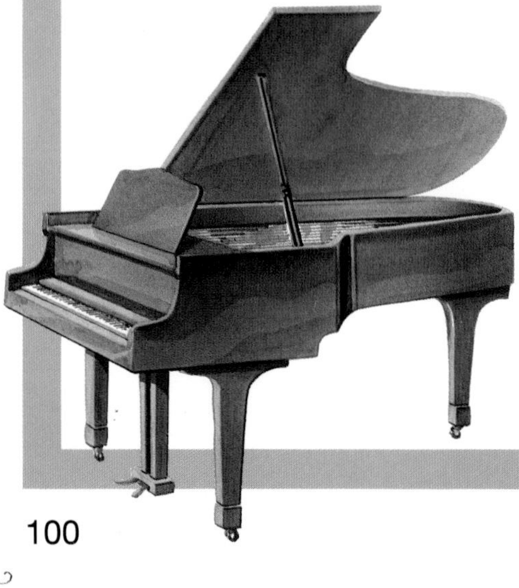

◁ You blow across the hole at the top of a **flute** and press the buttons with your fingers.

tambourine

triangle

move (moving, moved)

To **move** means to go from one place to another. *Don't **move**—I want to take your photograph.*

movie

A story told with a moving picture is called a **movie**.

mud

Mud is soft, wet earth.
*When we came home from playing in the field, we were covered in **mud**.*

multiply (multiplies, multiplying, multiplied)

To **multiply** a number, you add it to itself a given number of times.

*Two **multiplied** by four is eight.*

muscle *say *mussel*

Your **muscles** are the stretchy parts under your skin. They get tight and loose to help you move.

museum

A **museum** is a building where a lot of interesting things are on show for people to look at. *We saw the bones of a dinosaur in the **museum**.*

mushroom

A **mushroom** is a small, special kind of plant without leaves, shaped like an umbrella. *People eat some kinds of **mushrooms**.*

music

Music is sound that come from somebody singing or from a **musical instrument**, like a piano or a guitar. *We learn a lot of songs in **music** lessons at school.*

musician

A person who makes **music** is called a **musician**.

mystery (mysteries)

A **mystery** is something strange that has happened that people cannot explain.

Nn

nail

1 Your **nails** are the hard, shiny parts that cover the ends of your fingers and toes.
2 A **nail** is also a short piece of metal with a point at one end. You hit a **nail** with a hammer to attach one thing to another.

name

A **name** is what you call somebody or something. *My friends' names are David and Rosa.*

narrow

Something that is **narrow** has two sides that are not far apart. *The door of our house is very narrow.*

nation

A **nation** is all of the people who live in a country.

natural

Something that is **natural** has not been made by people. *Wood is a natural material, but plastic is not.*

nature

1 **Nature** is everything in the world that was not made by people. *We should do more to protect nature, not damage it.*
2 A person or an animal's **nature** is what they are really like. *Samantha is a nice girl—she has a kind nature.*

navy

A **navy** is all the ships belonging to a nation.

near

Something that is **near** is not far away. *I like sitting near the window.*

nearly

Nearly means not quite. *Sapphire is nearly as tall as Bobby.*

neat

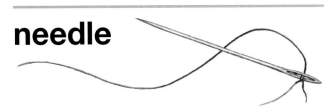

Neat means not messy. *Fold your clothes and put them in a **neat** pile.*

neck

Your **neck** is the part of your body that joins your head to your shoulders.

need (needing, needed)

If you **need** something, you must have it. *All plants and animals **need** water to live.*

needle

1 A **needle** is a long, thin, pointed piece of metal that you use for sewing. It has a hole at the top that thread goes through. Another kind of **needle** is used for knitting.
2 A **needle** is also a thin, sharp, green leaf. Some kinds of trees, like pines, have **needles**.

neighbor

A **neighbor** is somebody who lives near you. **Neighbors** live in a **neighborhood**.

Some words, such as **knee**, sound as though they begin with **n**, but you will find them in the dictionary under **kn**.

nephew

Somebody's **nephew** is the son of their brother or sister.

nest

A **nest** is a home that an animal makes for its young. *Birds build **nests** out of things like grass, mud, and sticks.*

net

A **net** is pieces of string tied together so that there are holes in between. People use **nets** to catch fish. **Nets** are also used in games like tennis and ice hockey.

never

Never means not at any time. *I have **never** seen a giraffe.*

new

1 Something that is **new** has never been used before. *My mom bought me some **new** shoes yesterday.*
2 **New** also means different. *We have a **new** swimming teacher this year.*

news

News is information about things that have just happened. *Have you heard the **news**? Katie has a new baby brother.*

newspaper

A **newspaper** is sheets of paper printed with words and pictures about things that are going on in the world.

next

Next means the one that comes after this one. ***Next** Saturday we are going to the beach.*

nice

If something or somebody is **nice**, they make you feel good or you like them. *This apple tastes **nice**.*

niece

Somebody's **niece** is the daughter of their brother or sister.

night

Another word that sounds like **night** is **knight**.

Night is the part of the day when the sky is dark and the Sun does not shine. People sleep at **night**.

Some words, such as **knife**, sound like they begin with **n**, but you will find them in the dictionary under **kn**.

nightmare

A **nightmare** is a frightening dream.

nod (nodding, nodded)

When you **nod**, you move your head up and down quickly as a way of saying "yes."

noise

A **noise** is a sound that somebody or something makes. *I heard a strange **noise** outside my window.*

noisy (noisier, noisiest)

Somebody or something that is **noisy** makes a lot of noise. *Don't be so **noisy**— you will wake up the baby!*

noon

Noon is 12 o'clock in the middle of the day.

normal

Normal means usual or ordinary. *Will you be home at the **normal** time today?*

north

North is a direction. If you look toward the Sun as it comes up in the morning, **north** is on your left.

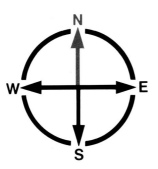

nose

Your **nose** is the part of your face you use for breathing and smelling.

Another word that sounds like **nose** is **knows**.

note

1 A **note** is a short letter to somebody. *Sarah left me a note saying she had gone swimming.*

I've gone swimming, back before dinner, Sarah

2 A **note** is also a sound in music that you can play or sing.

notice

1 (noticing, noticed) If you **notice** something, you see it and think about it. *Nadia noticed that Jamie was wearing a new coat.*
2 A **notice** is a piece of paper or a sign with writing on it which tells people something. *The notice said:* No dogs allowed.

now

Now means at this moment. *You are reading this book now.*

number

We use **numbers** when we count. 1, 2, and 3 are **numbers**. You can also write **numbers** as words (one, two, three).

nurse

A **nurse** is a person whose job is to look after people who are sick or hurt.

nut

A **nut** is a fruit that grows inside a very hard shell. *Peanuts and hazelnuts are different kinds of nuts.*

Word play
Trace this puzzle, then write in the answers using the pictures as clues.

Across 1

3   4

Down

1

2

3

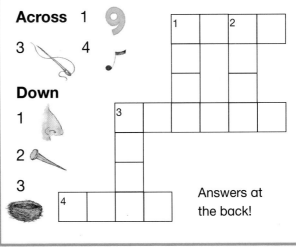

Answers at the back!

105

oar

An **oar** is a long piece of wood with one flat end that you use for moving a boat through water.

Another word that sounds like **oar** is **or**.

obey (obeying, obeyed)

When you **obey** somebody, you do what that person tells you to do. *When I tell my dog to sit, he always **obeys** me.*

ocean

An **ocean** is a very big sea. *The Pacific and the Atlantic are **oceans**.*

o'clock

O'clock is a word that you use to say what time it is. *I get up at eight **o'clock** in the morning.*

octopus
(octopuses)

An **octopus** is an animal that lives in the sea. It has eight long arms, called tentacles.

odd

1 An **odd** number is any number that ends in 1, 3, 5, 7, or 9. You cannot divide these numbers by 2 without something left over. The opposite of **odd** is even.
2 (odder, oddest)
If something is **odd**, it is strange. *My bike is making an **odd** noise —I think it needs oil.*
3 Odd things do not belong together in a pair or in a set. *Catrin is wearing **odd** socks!*

office

An **office** is a place where people go to work. **Offices** have things like desks, chairs, and computers.

often

If you do something **often**, you do it many times. *We **often** go shopping on Saturday mornings.*

oil

1 Oil is a smooth, thick liquid that comes from the ground. You can burn **oil** to make heat or to make machines move.
2 Oil is also a smooth liquid that people use for cooking. It comes from plants or animals.

old

1 Somebody who is **old** has lived for a long time. *My grandfather is very old—he is ninety!*
2 Something that is **old** was made a long time ago. *Our house is very old. It was built two hundred years ago.*
3 You also use **old** to talk about something that you had before. *My old school was farther from home than my new one.*

onion

An **onion** is a round vegetable with a strong taste and smell.

only

Only means no more than. *There is only one chocolate left in the box.*

open

1 If something like a door or a gate is **open**, you can go through it.
2 If something like a box is **open**, it is not closed or covered, so that you can see inside.

opposite

1 Opposite means different in every way. *Good is the opposite of bad, and hot is the opposite of cold.* (Look at the next page.)
2 Opposite also means on the other side. *Paulo is sitting opposite Jenna.*

orange

An **orange** is a round, sweet fruit with a thick skin.

orchestra

An **orchestra** is a large group of people playing different musical instruments together.

Opposites

closed / open

high / low

light / heavy

clean / dirty

happy / sad

little / big

old / young

long / short

hard / soft

Here are some more opposites. If you need to check
their meanings, you can find them all in this dictionary.

rough / smooth	thick / thin	hot / cold
cheap / expensive	fat / thin	tall / short
deep / shallow	new / old	loud / quiet
tight / loose	fast / slow	empty / full
wide / narrow	dry / wet	light / dark

order

1 Order means the way that things follow one another. *The letters of the alphabet always come in the same **order**.*
2 (ordering, ordered) If you **order** something, you say you would like it. *In the restaurant we **ordered** hamburgers and drinks.*
3 If you **order** somebody to do something, you say that they must do it. *The doctor **ordered** Michael to stay in bed.*

ordinary

Something that is **ordinary** is not exciting or special in any way. *Yesterday was my birthday, but today is just an **ordinary** day.*

ostrich (ostriches)

An **ostrich** is a large bird with long legs and a long neck. **Ostriches** cannot fly.

otter

An **otter** is a small animal with brown fur. **Otters** can swim very well and they catch fish to eat.

oval

Something that is **oval** is shaped like an egg.

oven

An **oven** is the part inside a stove where you put food to cook it.

over

Over means above. *I threw the ball **over** my friend's head.*

owe (owing, owed)

If you **owe** somebody something, you must give it to them. *Jamie lent me $1 for an ice cream cone yesterday, so I **owe** him $1.*

owl

An **owl** is a bird that hunts small animals at night.

Owls have large, round eyes and they can see well in the dark.

own (owning, owned)

If you **own** something, it belongs to you. *Do you know who **owns** that car?*

Pp

pack (packing, packed)

When you **pack** a bag or a box, you put clothes and other things inside it.

package

A **package** is a box or large envelope that you send in the mail.

paddle

A **paddle** is a short oar that you use for moving small boats through water.

page

A **page** is one side of a piece of paper in a book. *This book has a lot of pages.*

paid Look at **pay.**

pain

A **pain** is the feeling that you have in a part of your body when it hurts. *I have a pain in my stomach.*

paint

1 Paint is a liquid that we use to make pictures or to put color on something.
2 (painting, painted) When you **paint** a picture, you make a picture using paints. *Gemma is painting a rainbow.*
3 (painting, painted) When you **paint** something like a wall, you put paint on it. *I helped Mom paint the door red.*

painting

A **painting** is a picture that somebody has painted. *The teacher put our paintings up on the wall.*

pair

1 A **pair** is two things that you use together, like shoes. *I have a new pair of gloves.*
2 You also use **pair** to talk about things that have two parts the same joined together, like scissors or shoes.

Another word that sounds like **pair** is **pear.**

pajamas

Pajamas are a loose shirt and pants that you sleep in. *My pajamas have moons and stars on them.*

pale

Something that is **pale** is almost white. *You look very **pale**—are you feeling sick?*

palm

Your **palm** is the flat inside part of your hand between your fingers and your wrist.

pan

A **pan** is a metal container with a handle. You use it for cooking food in.

pancake

A **pancake** is a thin, round cake made from flour, eggs, and milk and cooked in hot oil in a pan.

panda

A **panda** is a black and white animal that looks like a bear. **Pandas** come from China.

pants

Pants are a piece of clothing that covers you from the waist down. Each leg goes inside a leg of the **pants**.

paper

Paper is thin sheets made from wood or cloth for writing on or for wrapping things in. *This book is made of **paper**.*

parachute

A **parachute** is a thing like a big umbrella made of light, strong cloth. It lets people float slowly down through the air when they jump out of an airplane.

parade

A **parade** is a group of people who walk down the street together. *Are you coming to the Memorial Day **parade**?*

parent

A **parent** is a mother or a father.

park

1 A **park** is a place with grass and trees where anybody can go to walk or play games. *We had a picnic in the **park**.*

2 (parking, parked) When somebody **parks** a car, they stop and leave it somewhere for a short time. *Ian **parked** outside the school.*

parrot

A **parrot** is a bird with brightly colored feathers. Many people keep **parrots** as pets. Some **parrots** can learn to talk.

part

A **part** is a piece of something. *Your hands and your head are **parts** of your body.*

party (parties)

A **party** is a group of people having fun together. *We went to Rosie's birthday **party** on Saturday.*

pass (passes, passing, passed)

1 If you **pass** somebody or something, you go by them. *Do you **pass** any stores on your way to school?*
2 When you **pass** something to somebody, you give it to them. *Please could you **pass** me the scissors?*

passenger

A **passenger** is a person who is traveling in a car, bus, train, ship, or an airplane.

past

1 The **past** is the time before now. *In the past, people did not have cars.*
2 **Past** also means after. *It's twelve minutes past six.*

pat

When you **pat** something, you tap it gently with your hand.

patch

A **patch** is a small piece of material used to cover a hole, a tear, or a crack in something.

path

A **path** is a narrow piece of land for people to walk along. *There is a **path** through the park.*

patient

1 A **patient** is a person who is sick and who is being looked after by a doctor or a nurse.
2 If you are **patient**, you can wait for something to happen without getting cross. *Just be **patient**—it will soon be your turn.*

pattern

A **pattern** is how lines, colors, and shapes look on something. *These pieces of paper have different **patterns** on them.*

paw

A **paw** is an animal's foot. *A cat has four paws.*

pay (pays, paying, paid)

When you **pay** somebody, you give them money for something. *My dad paid the driver for taking us home.*

pea

A **pea** is a small, round, green vegetable. **Peas** grow in long, green things called pods.

peace

Peace is a time when it is quiet, without any wars or fighting.

Another word that sounds like **peace** is **piece**.

peach (peaches)

A **peach** is a soft, round fruit with a yellow and red skin and a pit in the middle.

peacock

A **peacock** is a large, male bird with beautiful long blue and green feathers in its tail. The female is called a peahen.

peanut

A **peanut** is a nut with a light brown shell. **Peanuts** grow under the ground.

pear

A **pear** is a fruit that is green or yellow on the outside and white on the inside.

Another word that sounds like **pear** is **pair**.

pebble

A **pebble** is a small, round, smooth stone. *You often see pebbles on beaches.*

pedal

A **pedal** is a part of a machine that you press with your feet to make it move or work. *A bike has pedals.*

peel

1 Peel is the skin on some fruits and vegetables. *Apples, oranges, and potatoes all have **peel**.*
2 (peeling, peeled) If you **peel** something, you take the skin off it. *Rosa and Thomas are **peeling** some fruit.*

pen

A **pen** is a long, thin tool filled with ink that you use for writing.

pencil

A **pencil** is a long, thin stick with gray or colored lead in the middle. You use it for writing or drawing.

penguin

A **penguin** is a large black and white bird that lives in very cold parts of the world.
Penguins can swim well, but they cannot fly.

people

Men, women, and children are **people**.

pepper

1 Pepper is a powder with a hot taste that you can put on food.
2 A **pepper** is a bright red, green, or yellow vegetable. *I'd like **peppers** on my pizza.*

perch (perches, perching, perched)

To **perch** means to sit on the edge of something. *Birds often **perch** on branches.*

perfect

Something **perfect** has nothing wrong with it.

person

A **person** is a man, a woman, or a child.

pet

A **pet** is an animal like a dog, a hamster, or a goldfish that you keep and look after in your home. *Do you have any **pets**?*

petal

Petals are the soft, thin, colored parts of a flower.

phone

Phone is short for **telephone**.

photograph

A **photograph** is a picture that you take with a camera. The short word for **photograph** is **photo**.

piano (pianos)

A **piano** is a large musical instrument. It has black and white keys that you press to make sounds. *My brother is learning to play the piano.*

pick (picking, picked)

1 When you **pick** something, you take it because it is the one that you want. ***Pick the color that you like best.***
2 If you **pick** flowers or fruit, you take them from the place where they are growing. *We **picked** apples from the tree in the yard.*
3 When you **pick** something up, you lift it. *I bent down to **pick** up my pencil from the floor.*

picnic

A **picnic** is a meal that you take with you and eat outside. *We had a **picnic** by the river.*

picture

A **picture** is a drawing, a painting, or a photograph.

pie

A **pie** is fruit or meat covered with pastry and cooked in an oven. I like apple **pie** with ice cream.

piece

A **piece** is a part of something. *Would you like a **piece** of cake?*

Another word that sounds like **piece** is **peace**.

pig

A **pig** is an animal that is kept on farms. **Pigs** are fat and they have short legs, flat noses, and curly tails. A young **pig** is called a piglet.

pigeon

A **pigeon** is a bird with a small head and a large, round body. ***Pigeons** live in towns.*

pile

A **pile** is a lot of things on top of one another.

Sapphire has a big pile of books.

pill

A **pill** is a small, round piece of medicine that you swallow. *The doctor gave my mom some pills when she was sick.*

pillow

A **pillow** is a soft cushion that you put your head on when you are in bed.

pilot

A **pilot** is a person who flies an airplane.

pin

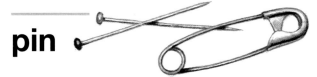

A **pin** is a small, thin piece of metal with a sharp point at one end. **Pins** are used for holding pieces of cloth together.

pipe

A **pipe** is a long tube that carries things like water, oil, or gas from one place to another.

pirate

A **pirate** is a person who robs ships at sea.

pizza

A **pizza** is a flat, round food that is baked in an oven. It is a kind of bread with tomato sauce, cheese, and other things on top.

place

A **place** is an area or a building where something is. *We took photos of all the places we visited on our vacation.*

plain

Something that is **plain** is all one color and has no pattern on it. *Lily is wearing a plain blue dress.*

Another word that sounds like **plain** is **plane**.

plan (planning, planned)

When you **plan** something, you decide what you are going to do and how to do it. *We are planning what to do over summer vacation.*

plane

A **plane** is a machine that flies. **Planes** have wings and engines. **Plane** is short for **airplane**.

Another word that sounds like **plane** is **plain**.

planet

A **planet** is a big, round thing in space that moves around a star. Earth is one of the nine **planets** traveling around the Sun. (Look at the next page.)

plant

1 A **plant** is anything that grows in earth. Trees and flowers are **plants**.
2 A **plant** is also a factory.

plaster

Plaster is soft stuff that gets hard when it dries. **Plaster** is used to cover walls and ceilings inside buildings. *Dad covered the hole in the wall with **plaster**.*

plastic

Plastic is a strong, light material that is made in factories. **Plastic** is used to make many different things.

plate

A **plate** is a round, flat thing that you put food on.

play

1 (playing, played) When you **play**, you do something to enjoy yourself. *We are **playing** in the yard. Do you want to **play** a game with us?*
2 (playing, played) When you **play** a musical instrument, you make sounds with it. *I'm learning to **play** the guitar.*
3 (plays) A **play** is a story that you watch on television or in the theater, or act out at school.

playground

A **playground** is a place outside where children can play.

Wordplay
Fix the broken plates and make some words for things to eat.

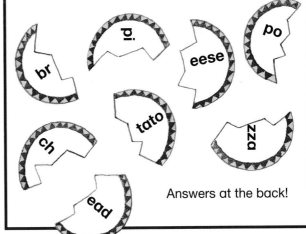

Answers at the back!

Planets

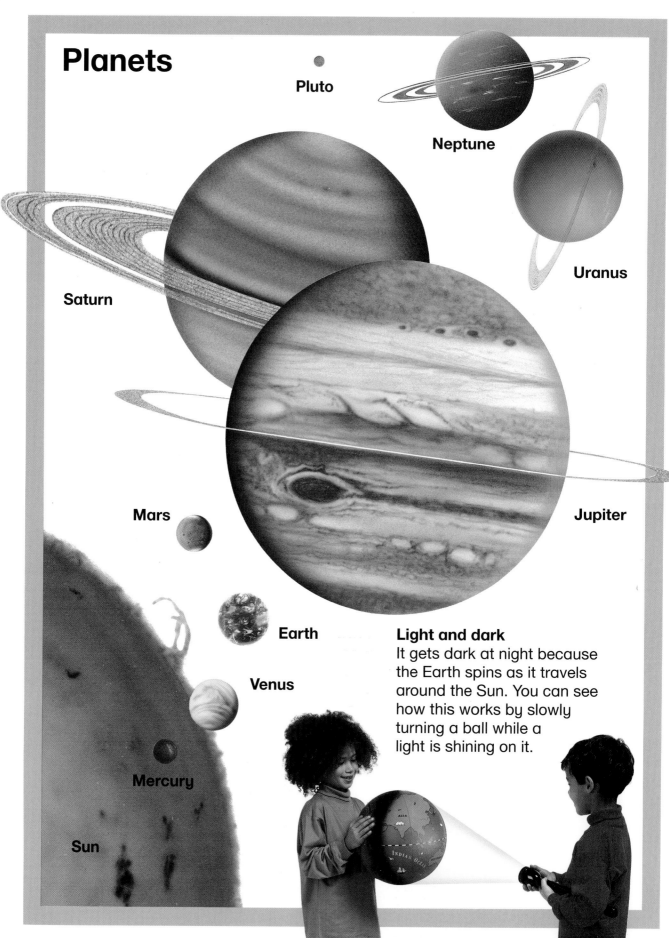

Pluto

Neptune

Uranus

Saturn

Jupiter

Mars

Earth

Venus

Mercury

Sun

Light and dark
It gets dark at night because the Earth spins as it travels around the Sun. You can see how this works by slowly turning a ball while a light is shining on it.

please

You say **please** when you are asking somebody to do something. *Please can you close the door?*

plenty

If there is **plenty** of something, there is more than you need. *Why don't you stay for dinner? There is **plenty** of food.*

plus

You use **plus** to talk about adding numbers together. *Four **plus** two is six.*

pocket

A **pocket** is a small bag that is sewn into clothes. **Pockets** are for putting things in.

poem

A **poem** is a piece of writing. **Poems** usually have short lines, and the last words of the lines often rhyme.

point

1 A **point** is the sharp end of something, like a pin or a pencil.
2 You get a **point** in a game when you score. *Our team got ten points*.
3 (pointing, pointed) If you **point**, you show where something is by using your finger.

pointed

Something that is **pointed** has a sharp end. *The witch is wearing a long, **pointed** hat.*

poisonous

Something that is **poisonous** can kill you or make you sick if you eat it. *Don't pick those berries because they are **poisonous**.*

polar bear

A **polar bear** is a big, white bear that lives in very cold parts of the world in the north.

pole

A **pole** is a long, thin piece of wood or metal. *The tent is held in place by metal poles*.

police

The **police** are people whose job is to make sure that everybody obeys the law.

polite

If you are **polite**, you behave well and you are not rude. *It is **polite** to say "thank you" when somebody gives you something.*

pond

A **pond** is a small lake. *The **pond** at the end of our street has fish and frogs in it.*

pony (ponies)

A **pony** is a kind of small horse.

pool

A **pool** is an area filled with water for swimming in.

poor

Somebody who is **poor** does not have a lot of money.

popcorn

Popcorn is a food made from a kind of corn that bursts open when you cook it.

porch

A **porch** is an area with a floor and a roof on the outside of a house. *When it is raining, we play on the **porch**.*

possible

Something that is **possible** can be done. *It is **possible** to fly faster than the speed of sound.*

post

A **post** is a strong pole that stands up in the ground.

post office

A **post office** is a building where you can buy stamps and send letters and packages.

pot

A **pot** is a deep, round container. *Dad made soup in a big **pot**. We grow plants in **pots**.*

potato (potatoes)

A **potato** is a vegetable that grows under the ground. **Potatoes** are brown on the outside and white on the inside.

pour (pouring, poured)

When you **pour** a liquid, you make it run out of a container. *Jenna is **pouring** some milk into the bowl.*

powder

A **powder** is something that is made up of a lot of very small pieces. *Flour is a **powder** and so is dust.*

power

Power is the strength to make something happen. *Cars get the **power** to move from gas.*

practice (practicing, practiced)

When you **practice** something, you do it lots of times so that you get better at it. *If you want to play the guitar well, you need to **practice** every day.*

prepare (preparing, prepared)

If you **prepare** something, you get it ready. *I helped my dad **prepare** dinner.*

present

1 A **present** is something that you give to somebody.

*I gave Paul a **present** for his birthday.*

2 The **present** is now. *I'm too busy to help you at **present**.*

president

A **president** is a person that other people have chosen to lead a country or company.

press (presses, pressing, pressed)

When you **press** something, you push hard on it. *You **press** these keys to play a tune.*

pretend (pretending, pretended)

If you **pretend**, you try to make people believe something that is not true. *Andrew is **pretending** to be asleep.*

pretty (prettier, prettiest)

Somebody or something that is **pretty** is nice to look at. *Flowers are **pretty**.*

price

The **price** of something is how much money you have to pay for it.

*The **price** of the lamp is written on the label.*

prince

A **prince** is the son or the grandson of a king or a queen.

princess (princesses)

A **princess** is the daughter or the granddaughter of a king or a queen.

print (printing, printed)

When somebody **prints** words and pictures, they put them on to paper using a machine. *This book was **printed**.*

prison

A **prison** is a building where people have to stay because they have done something that is against the law.

prize

A **prize** is something that people win for doing well. *Lucy won first **prize** for her painting.*

problem

A **problem** is something that is difficult to understand, decide, or answer. *If you have any **problems**, ask somebody to help you.*

program

A **program** is something that you watch or listen to on television or radio. *Did you see that **program** about snakes on television last night?*

project

A **project** is a piece of work that you do at school. You find out all about something and write about it. *Our class is doing a **project** on pets.*

promise (promising, promised)

When you **promise**, you say that you will or will not do something. *If I tell you what I'm going to give Hassan for his birthday, will you **promise** not to tell him?*

protect (protecting, protected)

To **protect** something means to keep it safe. *Gemma is wearing goggles to **protect** her eyes when she goes swimming.*

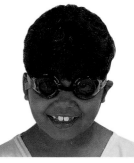

proud

If you are **proud**, you are pleased about something good that you have done or about something that is yours. *Sam is very **proud** of his new bike.*

prove (proving, proved or proven)

When you **prove** something, you show that it is true. *Scientists have **proved** that the Earth is round.*

pudding

A **pudding** is a soft, sweet cooked dessert. *My favorite dessert is rice **pudding**.*

puddle

A **puddle** is a small amount of liquid on the ground. *Don't step in that **puddle**!*

pull (pulling, pulled)

When you **pull** something, you hold it and move it toward you.

pumpkin

A **pumpkin** is a large, round orange fruit used for making pies and other food.

punish (punishes, punishing, punished)

To **punish** somebody means to make them sorry because they have done something wrong. *Ben's mom **punished** him for telling lies by sending him to bed early.*

pupil

A **pupil** is somebody who is learning something at school. *There are twenty-five **pupils** in my class.*

puppet

A **puppet** is a kind of doll that can be made to move. Some **puppets** have a space inside where you can put your hand. Others have strings that you pull.

puppy (puppies)

A **puppy** is a young dog. *Our dog has just had three **puppies**.*

pure

Something that is **pure** is not mixed with anything else. *The king's crown was made of **pure** gold.*

purse

A **purse** is a small bag that people keep money and other things in.

push (pushes, pushing, pushed)

When you **push** something, you move it away from you. *Ella is **pushing** her new toy around.*

puzzle

A **puzzle** is a game, a question, or a toy that you have fun trying to work out.

*My favorite thing to do on a rainy day is to sit down with a crossword **puzzle**.*

Qq

quack (quacking, quacked)

When a duck **quacks**, it makes a loud noise.

quarter

A **quarter** is one of four equal parts of something. A quarter is also a 25¢ coin, a **quarter** of $1.

queen

A **queen** is a woman who rules a country or the wife of a king.

question

You ask a **question** when you want to find out about something. *I asked my teacher a **question** about when dinosaurs lived.*

question mark

A **question mark** is the mark **?** used at the end of a written sentence to show that it is a question. *Do you know what I mean**?***

quick

1 If somebody or something is **quick**, they move fast. *Be **quick** or we'll miss the beginning of the movie.*
2 Quick also means done in a short time. *We only had time for a **quick** lunch because we were late.*

quiet

When somebody or something is **quiet**, they make a small amount of noise or no noise at all. *Be **quiet** or you will wake up the baby!*

quite

1 Quite means more than a little bit. *It's **quite** hot today.*
2 Not **quite** means almost. *Dinner is not **quite** ready.*

quiz (quizzes)

In a **quiz**, somebody asks a lot of questions to find out how much you know. *Our teacher gave us a **quiz** on the state capitals.*

Rr

rabbit

A **rabbit** is a small, wild animal with long ears and soft fur. *Some people keep rabbits as pets.*

race

You have a **race** to find out who or what can go the fastest. *Michael won the race.*

radio (radios)

A **radio** is an instrument that picks up waves sent through the air and turns them into sound. You turn on a **radio** to listen to music, news, and other programs.

raft

A **raft** is a kind of flat boat. **Rafts** are often made of lots of pieces of wood joined together.

railroad

A **railroad** is a kind of path made of metal bars for trains to run along.

rain

1 Rain is water that falls from the clouds in small drops.
2 (raining, rained) When it is **raining**, drops of water are falling from the sky.

rainbow

A **rainbow** is a curve of different colors that you sometimes see in the sky when the Sun shines after it has rained.

raise (raising, raised)

When you **raise** something, you lift it up. *If you know the answer to the question, please raise your hand.*

rake

A **rake** is a tool that you use outdoors. Some **rakes** are used for collecting leaves and grass into piles and others are used for making the earth smooth.

ran Look at **run**.

rang Look at **ring**.

rat

A **rat** is
an animal
that looks
like a big mouse.
Rats have long tails
and sharp teeth.

rattle (rattling, rattled)

To **rattle** means to make the sound of
things knocking together. *The coins **rattled**
in the can.*

raw

Food that is **raw** has not been cooked.
*Salads are usually made of **raw** vegetables.*

reach
(reaching, reached)

1 When you **reach**
for something, you
put your hand out
toward it.

*Eden is not tall enough
to **reach** the ceiling.*

2 When you **reach** a
place, you arrive
there. *It was very late
when we **reached**
Grandma's house.*

read *say reed
(reading, read *say red)

When you **read**, you look
at words and understand
what they mean.

*Omer is **reading** an
interesting book.*

ready

If you are **ready**, you can do something
right away. *We'll go out to play as soon as
you are **ready**.*

real

Something that is **real** is true or it is not a
copy. *This isn't a **real** spider. It's made of
plastic.*

really

Really means that something is true. *Did
the magician **really** make the rabbit
disappear or was it just a trick?*

reason

A **reason** explains why something happens
or why you do something. *The **reason** why
we're late is that we missed the bus.*

record

1 A **record** is a flat, round piece of plastic
that plays music or other sounds when it
turns on a record player.
2 A **record** is also the best that has ever
been done. *What is the world **record** for
running a mile?*

rectangle

A **rectangle** is a shape with two long sides, two shorter sides, and four corners. *This page is a rectangle.*

refrigerator

A **refrigerator** is a big metal box where you can put food to keep it cold and fresh. A short word for **refrigerator** is **fridge**.

refuse (refusing, refused)

If you **refuse**, you say you will not do something that somebody has asked you to do. *Dad asked my sister to clean her room but she refused.*

reindeer
(reindeer)

A **reindeer** is a large deer that lives in cold countries.

remember (remembering, remembered)

If you **remember** something, you keep it in your mind or bring it back into your mind. *Can you remember what you did on your birthday last year?*

remind (reminding, reminded)

To **remind** means to make somebody remember something. *Can you remind me to phone David tomorrow?*

repeat (repeating, repeated)

If you **repeat** something, you do it or say it again. *Could you repeat what you said? I didn't hear you the first time.*

reply (replies, replying, replied)

When you **reply**, you give an answer. *"Where have you been?" "Swimming," she replied.*

lizard

snake

tortoise

reptile

A **reptile** is an animal that has cold blood and skin covered in scales. **Reptiles** lay eggs. Snakes, tortoises and lizards are **reptiles**.

rescue
(rescuing, rescued)

If you **rescue** somebody, you save them from danger. *The helicopter rescued the man whose boat had sunk.*

rest

1 When you have a **rest**, you stop what you are doing for a time because you are tired. *Maria needed a **rest** after working hard in the garden all morning.*

2 The **rest** is what is left after a part of something has been taken away. *I ate half of the orange and gave the **rest** to my friend.*

restaurant

A **restaurant** is a place where people go to buy and eat meals. *We went to a **restaurant** on my dad's birthday.*

Wordplay
The box on the opposite page tells you that another word that sounds like **right** is **write**. Can you find another word that sounds like:

tail **hole** **way** **dear** **plane**

Look up these words in the dictionary if you need any help.

Answers at the back!

return (returning, returned)

1 When you **return**, you come back or go back. *When do you **return** to school after summer vacation?*

2 When you **return** something, you give it back. *I am going to **return** this book to the library when I have finished reading it.*

rhinoceros (rhinoceroses)

Rhinoceros comes from two Greek words that mean "nose horn."

A **rhinoceros** is a big, heavy, wild animal with a thick skin and one or two horns on its nose. **Rhinoceroses** live in Africa and Asia. They are called **rhinos** for short.

rhyme (rhyming, rhymed)

When words **rhyme**, they have the same sound at the end. *Red **rhymes** with bed, and house **rhymes** with mouse.*

ribbon

A **ribbon** is a long, thin piece of cloth or paper.

rice

Rice is a kind of food. It is the small, white seeds of a plant that get soft when they are cooked. **Rice** plants grow in wet ground in hot countries.

rich

Somebody who is **rich** has a lot of money. *If I were **rich**, I would live in a mansion and I would go everywhere by plane.*

ridden Look at **ride**.

riddle

A **riddle** is a strange question that has a funny or clever answer. *The answer to the **riddle** "What goes up when the rain comes down?" is "An umbrella."*

ride

1 (riding, rode, ridden) When you **ride** a horse or a bike, you sit on it as it moves along. *I love **riding** my new bike.*
2 When you take a **ride** in something like a car or a bus, you travel in it. *The farmer gave me a **ride** on his tractor.*

right

Another word that sounds like **right** is **write**.

1 Right is the opposite of left. *Rosa has a glove puppet on her **right** hand.*
2 If something is **right**, there are no mistakes. *I got all the answers **right**.*

ring

1 A **ring** is a small circle of metal that you wear around your finger.
2 A **ring** is also a circle with an empty center. *The children sat in a **ring** around the teacher.*
3 (ringing, rang, rung) To **ring** is to make the sound of a bell. *The telephone is **ringing**—will somebody please answer it?*

ripe

When fruit is **ripe**, it is ready to eat. *This banana is not **ripe** yet—it's still green.*

rise (rising, rose, risen)

To **rise** means to move up. *The Sun **rises** in the east every morning.*

river

A **river** is a lot of moving water with land on both sides. A **river** flows into a lake or into the sea.

road

A **road** is a wide path leading from one place to another for cars, trucks, buses, and bicycles to travel along.

Another word that sounds like **road** is **rode**.

roar (roaring, roared)

To **roar** means to make a loud noise like a lion makes. *We heard the plane's engines roar just before it took off.*

rob (robbing, robbed)

To **rob** means to take something that does not belong to you. *The men who robbed the bank stole thousands of dollars.*

robber

A **robber** is somebody who steals things from somebody or from a place.

robin

A **robin** is a bird with red feathers on the front of its body.

robot

A **robot** is a machine that can do some of the same work that people do. In factories, a lot of work is now done by **robots**.

rock

1 Rock is the very hard material that mountains are made of. Pieces of this are called **rocks**.
2 (rocking, rocked) If you **rock** something, you move it gently backward and forward or from side to side. *Dad rocked the baby in his arms.*

rocket

A **rocket** is a big machine for traveling into space. It is in the shape of a tube with burning gases inside that make it fly into the sky.

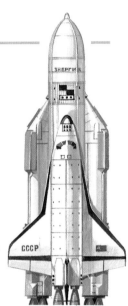

rode Look at ride.

Another word that sounds like **rode** is **road**.

roll

1 (rolling, rolled) When something like a ball **rolls**, it moves along by turning over and over. *Jenny rolled the ball down the hill.*
2 A **roll** of something like cloth or tape is a long piece of it that has been wrapped around itself lots of times.
3 A **roll** is also a round piece of bread for one person to eat. *I had two rolls with my dinner.*

Some words such as **wrong**, sound as though they begin with **r**, but you will find them in the dictionary under **wr**.

roof

A **roof** is the part on top that covers a building or something like a car or a bus.

room

1 A **room** is a part inside a building. Bedrooms and kitchens are **rooms**.
2 **Room** is also space. *There is not enough room in our car for ten people!*

rooster

A **rooster** is a male chicken.

root

The **roots** of a plant are the parts that grow under the ground.

rope

A **rope** is a very strong, thick string. People use **ropes** to lift and pull heavy things.

rose

1 A **rose** is a flower with lots of petals and sharp pointed parts called thorns on its stem. *Roses usually smell nice.*
2 Look at **rise**.

rough *say ruff

Something that is **rough** is not smooth. *A cat's tongue feels rough.*

round

1 Something that is **round** has the same shape as a circle or a ball.
2 **Round** also means on all sides of something. *The dancer twirled round and round on her toes.*

row *rhymes with go

1 A **row** is a line of people or things. *Our teacher asked us all to sit in a row.*
2 (rowing, rowed) When you **row** a boat, you move it along by using oars. *We rowed up the river.*

rub (rubbing, rubbed)

When you **rub** something, you move your hand or another thing backward and forward across it.

Felicity is rubbing a cloth across the board.

rubber

Rubber is a strong material that stretches and bounces and keeps out water. **Rubber** is made from the juice of a **rubber** tree. *Automobile tires are made out of black rubber.*

rude

If you are **rude** to someone, you are not polite or friendly to them.

ruby (rubies)

A **ruby** is a red jewel that is worth a lot of money.

rug

A **rug** is made of wool or material. You use it to cover part of a floor. *There is a **rug** beside my bed.*

ruin (ruining, ruined)

If something is **ruined**, it is spoiled. *The rain **ruined** our picnic.*

Wordplay

Match a picture clue on the left with one on the right to make four new words.

Answers at the back!

rule

1 A **rule** tells you that you must do something or that you must not do it. *In soccer it is against the **rules** to touch the ball with your hand.*
2 (ruling, ruled) To **rule** means to control a country and the people who live there. *The queen **ruled** her country well.*

ruler

1 A **ruler** is a piece of wood, metal, or plastic that you use for drawing or measuring straight lines.
2 A **ruler** is also a person who is the leader of a country.

rumble (rumbling, rumbled)

To **rumble** means to make a sound like thunder. *The big truck **rumbled** past.*

run (running, ran, run)

When you **run**, you go somewhere by moving your legs quickly.

*Robert had to **run** for the bus because he was late.*

rung Look at **ring**.

rush (rushing, rushed)

If you **rush**, you go somewhere or do something quickly. *We **rushed** home from school to play with our new puppy.*

Ss

sad (sadder, saddest)

If you are **sad**, you feel unhappy. *I felt sad when my best friend went away.*

safe

If you are **safe**, you are not in any danger. *The lost gerbil was found safe and well.*

said Look at **say**.

sail

A **sail** is a big piece of cloth on a boat. The wind blows against the **sail** and moves the boat along.

salad

A **salad** is a cold food made of different vegetables and other things mixed together.

salt

Salt is a white powder that people put on their food. *Sea water has salt in it.*

same

If two things are the **same**, they are just like each other.

Alice's socks are the same as José's.

sand

Sand is a kind of powder made of lots of very small pieces of rock. *You can see sand on the beach and in deserts.*

sandwich (sandwiches)

A **sandwich** is two slices of bread with food in between them. *I had a sandwich for lunch.*

sang Look at **sing**.

sank Look at **sink**.

sat Look at **sit**.

saucepan

A **saucepan** is a metal pot for cooking food. It has a lid and a long handle.

saucer

A **saucer** is a kind of small plate for putting a cup on.

save (saving, saved)

1 If you **save** somebody, you take them away from danger. *The man jumped into the river and **saved** the child.*

2 If you **save** money or something else, you keep it somewhere to use later. *I'm **saving** up for a new computer game.*

saw

1 Look at **see**.
2 A **saw** is a tool for cutting wood. It has a blade with sharp points like teeth along one edge.

say (saying, said)

When you **say** something, you make words with your mouth. *Lucy **said** she was sorry.*

scale

1 You use a **scale** or **scales** to find out how heavy somebody or something is.

*Joe stood on the **scale** to weigh himself.*

2 Scales are also the small, hard, flat things that cover the bodies of fish and reptiles.

scare (scaring, scared)

If something **scares** you, it makes you feel frightened. *The monster in the movie **scared** me when it suddenly appeared.*

scarecrow

A **scarecrow** is a thing that looks like a person dressed in old clothes. Farmers put **scarecrows** in their fields to frighten off birds.

scarf (scarves)

A **scarf** is a long piece of cloth that you wear around your neck.

school

A **school** is a place where children go to learn. *What did you do at **school** today?*

abcdefghijklmnopqrstuvwxyz

science

Science is something that you can learn about at school. **Science** teaches us about things like animals and plants as well as about the Earth and other planets. A scientist is a person who finds out how things happen in **science**.

scissors

You use **scissors** for cutting. A pair of **scissors** has two sharp parts joined together.

score

1 In a game, the **score** is how many points each side has. *At the end of the field hockey game the **score** was 4-2.*
2 (scoring, scored) To **score** means to get a point in a game. *In baseball, you **score** one point for each run.*

scratch

(scratches, scratching, scratched)

To **scratch** means to rub something sharp against something else. *The cat is **scratching** the tree with its sharp claws.*

scream (screaming, screamed)

If you **scream**, you call or shout in a loud voice.

screen

1 A **screen** is a flat surface on which a movie or a television picture is shown.
2 A **screen** is also a net with very small holes in it that fits over windows.

Another word that sounds like **sea** is **see**.

sea

A **sea** is a large area of salt water. Many fish live in the **sea**. *I like swimming in the **sea**.*

seal

A **seal** is an animal with short, gray fur that lives in the sea and on land. **Seals** eat fish.

search (searches, searching, searched)

When you **search** for something, you look very carefully for it.

seashore

The **seashore** is the land next to the sea. *We like swimming and playing in the sand when we go to the **seashore** for our vacation.*

season

The **seasons** are the four parts of the year. They are called spring, summer, autumn (also called fall), and winter.

seat

A **seat** is anything that you sit on. Buses and cars have **seats**. *We sat in the front **seats** when we went to see the movie.*

second

1 A **second** is a very short time. There are 60 **seconds** in a minute.
2 Second means next after the first. *Sam won the race and I came in **second**.*

secret

A **secret** is something that only a few people know about. *I can't tell you what's in the box. It's a **secret**!*

see (seeing, saw, seen)

When you **see** something, you notice it with your eyes. *My dad can't **see** well without his glasses.*

Another word that sounds like **see** is **sea**.

seed

A **seed** is a very small, hard part of a plant. **Seeds** are put in the ground, and new plants grow from them.

seem (seeming, seemed)

To **seem** means to look or feel like something. *Tara is tall, so she **seems** older than she really is.*

seen Look at **see**.

seesaw

A **seesaw** is a toy. It has a long, flat part that two people sit on, one at each end, to go up and down.

sell (selling, sold)

If somebody **sells** something to you, they give it to you and you pay money. *The woman was **selling** all kinds of vegetables.*

send (sending, sent)

When you **send** something somewhere, you make it go there. *I am **sending** this letter to my friend.*

Some words, such as **center**, sound as though they begin with **s**, but you will find them in the dictionary under **c**.

sent Look at **send**.

sentence

A **sentence** is a group of words. A **sentence** begins with a capital letter (like A, B, or C) and ends with a period (.).

serious

If you are **serious**, you are not being silly and you are telling he truth. *My dad was* **serious** *when he said we could go to the ball game.*

set

A **set** is a group of things that belong together. *I have a new train* **set**.

sew (sewing, sewed, sewn)

When you **sew**, you join pieces of cloth together or join something to cloth using a needle and thread.

Can you **sew** *this button back on my shirt, please?*

Another word that sounds like **sew** is **so**.

shade

Shade is a place that the sun doesn't shine on. *We sat in the shade of a tree.*

shadow

A **shadow** is a dark shape that you see near somebody or something that is in the way of the light.

shake (shaking, shook, shaken)

When you **shake** something, you move it quickly up and down or backward and forward.

shallow

Water that is **shallow** is not very deep. *I am learning to swim in the* **shallow** *end of the pool.*

shape

The **shape** of something is what you see if you draw a line around the outside of it. Circles, squares, and triangles are all different **shapes**. (Look at the next page.)

Shapes

square

triangle

rectangle

circle

semicircle

oval

hexagon

octagon

star

crescent

diamond

heart

cylinder

cube

cone

sphere

share (sharing, shared)

1 If you **share** something, you give a part of it to somebody else. *Alice is **sharing** her orange with her friends.*
2 To **share** also means to use something together with another person. *I **share** a bedroom with my sister.*

shark

A **shark** is a very big fish with many sharp teeth. ***Sharks** live in the sea.*

sharp

Something that is **sharp** has an edge or point that is good at cutting. *Knives and scissors are usually **sharp**.*

sheep (sheep)

A **sheep** is an animal that farmers keep for their thick wool and for their meat. A young **sheep** is called a lamb.

sheet

1 A **sheet** is a large piece of cloth for putting on a bed.
2 A **sheet** is also a thin, flat piece of something. *May I have a **sheet** of paper?*

shelf (shelves)

A **shelf** is a long, flat piece of wood stuck to a wall. You can put things on it.

shell

A **shell** is the hard outside part of something. Eggs, nuts, and snails have **shells**. The **shells** that you find on the beach once had animals living in them.

shelves Look at **shelf**.

shine (shining, shone)

When something **shines**, it gives out light, or it is bright like silver. *The sun is **shining**.* Something that is **shiny** is smooth and bright. *Our new car is very **shiny**.*

ship

A **ship** is a big boat for carrying people and things across the ocean.

shirt

You wear a **shirt** on the top part of your body. A **shirt** has parts that cover your arms, and usually a collar and buttons.

shoe

You wear **shoes** on your feet. **Shoes** are usually made of leather or plastic. *I am wearing blue shoes today.*

shone Look at shine.

shook Look at shake.

shoot (shooting, shot)

1 To **shoot** means to make something go forward from a thing like a bow or a gun. *You shoot arrows with a bow.*
2 To **shoot** also means to move somewhere very fast. *Patrick shot out of the room.*

shop

1 (shopping, shopped) To **shop** means to buy things. *We went shopping for food in the supermarket.*
2 A **shop** is a place where you go to buy things.

shore

The **shore** is the land along the edge of a body of water such as a lake or the ocean.

short

1 Something that is **short** is not very long. *My brother has short hair. I wrote my grandma a short letter.*
2 Somebody who is **short** is not very tall.

shot Look at shoot.

shoulder

Your **shoulder** is the top part of your arm where it joins your neck.

shout

(shouting, shouted)

When you **shout**, you say something very loudly.

Mia had to shout so that we could hear her.

show (showing, showed, shown)

1 When you **show** something, you let people see it. *Show me your photos.*
2 When you **show** somebody how to do something, you teach them how to do it. *I showed my brother how to tie a bow.*

shower

1 A **shower** is a place where you can wash yourself by standing under water that is coming down on you.
2 A **shower** is also rain that falls for only a short time.

shown Look at **show**.

shrink (shrinking, shrank, shrunk)

When something **shrinks**, it gets smaller. *These jeans **shrank** when they were washed.*

shut
(shutting, shut)

When you **shut** a door, window, book, or another thing, you move it so that it is not open. *Please **shut** the window.*

sick

When you are **sick**, you do not feel well.

side

1 The **side** of something is the left or right of it. *You can see the alphabet at the **side** of this page.*
2 The **sides** of something can also be its flat surfaces. *This box has six **sides**.*
3 The **sides** of something can also be the edges. *A square has four **sides**.*
4 The **sides** in a game are the teams that are playing against each other.

sign

1 A **sign** is anything with writing or a picture on it telling you something.
2 (signing, signed) When you **sign** your name, you write it. ***Sign** your name here.*

silence

Silence means that there are no sounds. *We waited in **silence** for the story to begin.*

silly (sillier, silliest)

If you say that somebody is being **silly,** you mean that they are not thinking carefully about what they are doing. *It was very **silly** of you to run across the road without looking.*

silver

Silver is a gray, shiny metal. Rings and necklaces are often made of **silver**.

sing (singing, sang, sung)

When you **sing**, you make music with your voice. ***Sing** that song again.*

sink

1 (sinking, sank, sunk) When something **sinks**, it goes down under water. *If you throw a stone into water, it will **sink**.*
2 A **sink** is something in the kitchen where you can wash the dishes.

sister

Your **sister** is a girl who has the same mother and father as you.

Some words, such as **city**, sound as though they begin with **s**, but you will find them in the dictionary under **c**.

sit (sitting, sat)

When you **sit** somewhere, you rest your bottom there. *Amy told her dog to **sit**.*

size

The **size** of something is how big it is. *What size shoes do you take? I take a **size** 7.*

skate

1 Skates are special boots with wheels on the bottom that you wear for moving around on smooth ground.
2 Skates are also boots with sharp blades on the bottom that you wear for moving around on ice.

ski

Skis are long, flat, narrow pieces of plastic, wood, or metal. You wear them with special boots to go fast on snow.

skin

Skin is what covers the outside of people, most animals, and many plants. *When you peel an orange, you take off its **skin**.*

skip
(skipping, skipped)

When you **skip**, you move with little jumps from one foot to the other.

*Mia is **skipping** with a rope.*

skirt

A **skirt** is something that girls and women wear. It hangs down from the waist. *Sara is wearing a blue **skirt**.*

skull

Your **skull** is the round bone of your head. *Your brain is inside your **skull**.*

sky

The **sky** is the space above the Earth. You can often see the Moon and the stars in the **sky** at night.

sled

A **sled** is something that you sit on to ride on the snow. It has two long pieces of metal on the bottom which help it to slide along.

sleep (sleeping, slept)

When you **sleep**, you close your eyes and rest your whole body. People usually **sleep** at night.

slice

A **slice** is a thin, flat piece that has been cut from something. *May I have a slice of bread and butter, please?*

slide

1 (sliding, slid) When something **slides**, it moves easily over another thing. *The snake slid along the ground.*
2 A **slide** is something that you play on. You climb up the steps on one side and then **slide** down the other side.

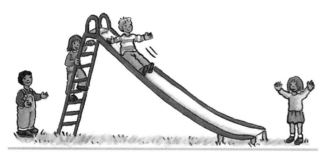

slip (slipping, slipped)

If you **slip**, you slide by mistake and fall down. *I slipped on the wet floor.*

slow

Somebody or something that is **slow** does not move quickly. *Turtles are very slow animals.*

small

Somebody or something that is **small** is not very big. *This shirt is too small for me.*

smash (smashes, smashed)

If something **smashes**, it breaks into a lot of pieces. *I dropped the plate and it smashed on the floor.*

smell (smelling, smelled)

1 When you **smell** something, you use your nose to find out about it. *Jenna is smelling a rose.*

2 When something **smells**, you find out about it using your nose. *A baking cake smells delicious.*

smile
(smiling, smiled)

When you **smile**, the corners of your mouth turn up to show that you are happy.

smoke

Smoke is the gray or black gas that goes up into the air when something is burning.

smooth

If something is **smooth**, you cannot feel any rough parts on it when you touch it. *The glass in a window is smooth.*

snail

A **snail** is a small creature with a hard shell on its back. **Snails** move along very slowly.

snake

A **snake** is a long, thin animal with no legs. It moves by sliding along the ground. **Snakes** are reptiles.

sneakers

Sneakers are cloth or leather shoes with rubber on the bottom. They are worn when playing sports.

sneeze (sneezing, sneezed)

When you **sneeze**, you blow air out of your nose and mouth with a sudden, loud noise. *You often **sneeze** when you have a cold.*

snow

Snow is small, white pieces of frozen water that fall from the sky when the weather is very cold. Each piece of **snow** is called a snowflake. *We like playing in the **snow**, making snowballs and building a snowman.*

soap

People use **soap** with water for washing themselves. *This bar of **soap** smells nice.*

sock

Socks are soft things that you wear inside your shoes to cover your feet, ankles, and sometimes the bottom part of your legs.

sofa

A **sofa** is a soft seat with arms and a back. Two or three people can sit on a **sofa**.

soft

Something that is **soft** is not hard or firm. *Kittens have **soft** fur.*

soil

Soil is the earth that plants grow in.

sold Look at **sell**.

solid

Something that is solid is hard and it has a shape. *This book is **solid**, but water is not.*

son

Somebody's **son** is a boy or a man who is their child.

Another word that sounds like **son** is **sun**.

song

A **song** is a piece of music with words that you sing.

sore

If a part of your body feels **sore**, it hurts. *My throat is **sore**.*

sorry

If you are **sorry**, you are sad about something. *I'm **sorry** I broke your pen.*

sort

A **sort** is a kind. *What **sort** of books do you like reading? I like adventure stories.*

sound

A **sound** is something that you can hear. *I heard the **sound** of a baby crying.*

soup

Soup is a hot liquid food made from things like vegetables or meat. *You eat **soup** with a spoon.*

sour

Something that is **sour** has a taste that is not sweet. Lemons and dill pickles are **sour**.

south

South is the direction that is on your right if you watch the Sun coming up in the morning.

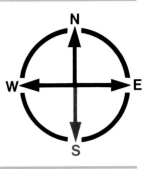

space

1 Space is a place that has nothing in it. *There is **space** here for you to put your box of toys.*

2 Space is also the sky around the Earth and farther away, where all the stars and planets are.

spaghetti

Spaghetti is a food made from wheat. It is in the shape of long strings. *I ordered **spaghetti** at the restaurant.*

speak (speaking, spoke, spoken)

When you **speak**, you say words. *I am **speaking** to my friend on the telephone.*

special

1 If something is **special**, it is better or more important than other things. *Today is a **special** day because it's my birthday.*
2 Special also means made to do a job. *You need a **special** camera for taking photos under water.*

spell

1 (spelling, spelled) When you **spell** a word, you say or write the letters in the right order. *"How do you **spell** 'spider'?"* *"S-p-i-d-e-r."*

2 A **spell** is a magic trick that you can read about in stories. *The fairy put a **spell** on the prince and turned him into a frog.*

spend (spending, spent)

1 When you **spend** money, you pay for something. *I have **spent** all my money on a present for my brother.*

2 When you **spend** time, you use that time to do something. *We **spent** our vacation at the beach.*

spider

A **spider** is a small creature with eight legs and no wings. **Spiders** spin webs to catch insects.

Spider comes from an old English word that meant "spinner."

Wordplay

Look at the pictures and spell the words. The first letter of each word is given to help you. Use the dictionary to check your answers if you need to.

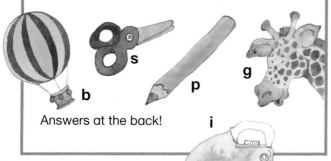

b

s

p

g

Answers at the back!

i

spill (spilling, spilled)

If you **spill** something, you make it flow out by mistake.

*I **spilled** my drink all over the floor.*

spin (spinning, spun)

1 When something **spins**, it turns around and around very fast. *My little brother likes to **spin** in circles.*

2 **Spin** also means to pull cotton, wool or something else into a long, thin piece and twist it to make thread.

splash (splashing, splashed)

To **splash** means to make somebody or something wet with drops of liquid. *My friend rode through a puddle on her bike and **splashed** us with dirty water.*

spoil (spoiling, spoiled)

If somebody **spoils** something, they make it less good than it was before. *I **spoiled** my new shirt when I spilled paint on it.*

spoke Look at **speak**.

spoken Look at **speak**.

spoon

A **spoon** is a small bowl with a long handle for eating things like soup and cereal.

sport

A **sport** is a game or something else that you do to keep your body strong and well and to have fun. *Football, tennis, and running are all **sports**.*

spot

1 A **spot** is a small, round mark. *Leopards have yellow fur with dark **spots**.*
2 A **spot** is also a small place. *This is a good **spot** for fishing.*

spring

1 Spring is the part of the year between winter and summer. *In the **spring**, plants start to grow again.*
2 A **spring** is a curly piece of metal that will jump back into the same shape if you press or pull it and then let it go.
3 (springing, sprang, sprung) To **spring** means to jump. *The cat **sprang** up onto the wall.*

spun Look at **spin**.

square

A **square** is a shape with four straight sides that are the same length.

squash (squashing, squashed)

If you **squash** something, you press it hard and make it flat.

squeeze
(squeezing, squeezed)

If you **squeeze** something, you press hard on the sides. *You **squeeze** a toothpaste tube to make the toothpaste come out.*

squirrel

A **squirrel** is a small animal with a big, thick tail. **Squirrels** live in trees.

stairs

Stairs are steps for going up or down inside a building.

Another word that sounds like **stairs** is **stares**.

stamp

A **stamp** is a small piece of paper with a picture and a price on it. *You have to stick a **stamp** on a letter before you send it.*

a b c d e f g h i j k l m n o p q r s t u v w x y z

stand (standing, stood)

When you **stand** somewhere, you are on your feet. *I am **standing** up because there is nowhere to sit.*

star

1 A **star** is a very small, bright light that you see in the sky at night.
2 A **star** is also a shape with five or six points.

stare (staring, stared)

When you **stare**, you look hard at something for a long time.

*It's rude to **stare** at people.*

Another word that sounds like **stares** is **stairs**.

start (starting, started)

When you **start**, you do the first part of something. *I am just **starting** to read my new book.*

station

A **station** is a place where trains stop so that people can get on and off. *We get off the train at the next **station**.*

statue

A **statue** is the shape of a person or an animal made of stone or metal.

stay (staying, stayed)

When you **stay** somewhere, you are there and you do not go away. *My sister got up early, but I **stayed** in bed until ten o'clock.*

steady (steadier, steadiest)

Something that is **steady** is not moving or shaking. *Hold the ladder **steady** while I climb up.*

steal (stealing, stole, stolen)

To **steal** means to take something that does not belong to you.

steam

When we see a cloud coming from hot liquid we call it **steam**.

stem

The **stem** of a plant is the long, thin part that grows above the ground.

step

1 When you take a **step**, you lift your foot and put it down in a different place.

2 Steps are also the flat part of stairs where you put your foot to go up or down.

stick

1 A **stick** is a long, thin piece of wood.
2 (sticking, stuck) When you **stick** something, you join it to something with glue or tape.
3 (sticking, stuck) When you **stick** a pointed thing like a pin into something else, you push it in. *If you **stick** a pin into a balloon, it will pop.*

still

1 If somebody or something is **still**, it is not moving. *Please stand **still** while I take your photograph.*
2 **Still** also means that something has not stopped. *It has been raining all day, and it is **still** raining now.*

sting (stinging, stung)

If an insect or a plant **stings** you, a small sharp point goes into your skin and hurts you. *Bees and wasps can **sting** you.*

stir (stirring, stirred)

When you **stir** something, you move something like a spoon around to mix it.

stole Look at steal.

stolen Look at steal.

stomach

Your **stomach** is the place inside your body where your food goes after you eat it.

stone

A **stone** is a small, smooth piece of rock. *My friends and I spent the afternoon skipping **stones** across the pond.*

stood Look at stand.

stop (stopping, stopped)

1 If you **stop** what you are doing, you do not do it anymore. *Please **stop** making so much noise.*

2 When something that was moving **stops**, it stands still.

store

1 (storing, stored) If you **store** something, you put it away to use later. *You can **store** eggs in the refrigerator.*
2 A **store** is also a building where you can buy things.

storm

A **storm** is very bad weather with strong winds and a lot of rain or snow. Many **storms** also have thunder and lightning.

story (stories)

A **story** tells you about things that happened. Some **stories** are about real things and others are made up.

stove

A **stove** is a machine used for cooking food.

straight

If something is **straight**, it does not bend, curl, or turn to the side. *You can use a ruler to draw a straight line.*

strange

1 Something that is **strange** is very different from what you expect. *I am drawing a picture of a strange animal. It would be strange if you didn't know your own name.*
2 A **strange** place is somewhere you have never been to before.

straw

1 Straw is the dry stems of plants like wheat. *The horse sleeps on straw.*
2 A **straw** is a long, thin tube made of paper or plastic for drinking through.

Paulo likes drinking through a straw.

stream

A **stream** is a small river. *The dog is jumping over the stream.*

street

A **street** is a road in a town with buildings along each side.

stretch (stretches, stretching, stretched)

If you **stretch** something, you make it longer or wider by pulling it. *Rosa's toy stretches.*

strict

If somebody is **strict**, they expect people to do what they say and to obey rules. *Our teacher is strict, but we like her.*

string

1 String is very thin rope. You use **string** for tying up things like packages.
2 Musical instruments like violins have wire **strings** that you play.

strip

A **strip** is a long, thin piece of something. *We are cutting the paper into **strips**.*

stripe

A **stripe** is a colored line on something.

strong

1 If you are **strong**, you have a lot of power. *Are you **strong** enough to lift this heavy box?*
2 If something is **strong**, you cannot break it easily.
3 If a taste or smell is **strong**, you can notice it easily. *This cheese has a very **strong** smell.*

stuck Look at **stick**.

student

A **student** is somebody who is learning something.

stung Look at **sting**.

submarine

A **submarine** is a boat that can travel under water.

subtract

(subtracting, subtracted)

To **subtract** means to take one number away from another. *If you **subtract** three from five you are left with two.*

subway

A **subway** is a train that runs in tunnels under city streets. *My mom rides the subway to work.*

sudden

Something that is **sudden** happens quickly and when you do not expect it. *There was a **sudden** loud noise.*

suddenly

Suddenly means quickly. *It was sunny all day and then **suddenly** it started to rain.*

sugar

Sugar is something that you put in food and drinks to make them sweet.

suit

A **suit** is a set of clothes that match because they are made out of the same cloth. A **suit** can be a jacket and pants, or a jacket and a skirt.

abcdefghijklmnopqrstuvwxyz

sum

A **sum** is the answer you get when you add numbers together.

Another word that sounds like **sum** is **some**.

summer

Summer is the hottest part of the year. It comes between spring and autumn.

Another word that sounds like **sun** is **son**.

Sun

The **Sun** is the big, bright star that we can see in the sky during the day. The **Sun** gives us light and keeps us warm.

sung Look at **sing**.

sunk Look at **sink**.

sunny (sunnier, sunniest)

When the Sun is shining brightly, it is **sunny**. *It's a sunny day today.*

sunshine

Sunshine is the light and heat from the Sun. *My cat likes sitting in the sunshine.*

supermarket

A **supermarket** is a big store where you can buy food and other things. You take what you want as you go around and then pay for everything on your way out.

supper

Supper is a meal that people eat in the evening.

sure

If you are **sure**, you know that something is right. *I am sure I know that boy.*

surface

The **surface** of something is the outside part. *The surface of the road is full of holes.*

surprise

A **surprise** is something that happens that you did not expect.

We baked a cake as a surprise for my brother's birthday.

swallow (swallowing, swallowed)

When you **swallow** food or drink, it goes down your throat.

swam Look at **swim**.

swan

A **swan** is a big, white bird that lives on water. A young **swan** is called a cygnet.

sweater

A **sweater** is something that covers the top part of your body and your arms to keep you warm. **Sweaters** are often made of wool.

sweep (sweeping, swept)

When you **sweep**, you clean a floor with a brush.

sweet

Sweet foods and drinks have a taste like sugar. *Ice cream is **sweet**.*

swept Look at **sweep**.

swim (swimming, swam, swum)

When you **swim**, you use your arms and legs to move your body through water. *I am going **swimming** this afternoon.*

swing

1 (swinging, swung) When something **swings**, it moves backward and forward through the air. *You **swing** your arms when you walk.*
2 A **swing** is a seat for swinging that hangs on two ropes or chains.

switch (switches)

A **switch** is something that you press or turn to stop or start something working. *You press this **switch** to turn on the television.*

swum Look at **swim**.

swung Look at **swing**.

Some words, such as **cycle**, sound as though they begin with **s**, but you will find them in the dictionary under **c**.

Wordplay
Can you find the names of nine animals hidden in this box?

b	s	h	e	e	p
a	n	t	o	r	a
t	a	s	w	a	n
o	k	x	l	t	d
z	e	b	r	a	a

Answers at the back!

abcdefghijklmnopqrs**t**uvwxyz

table

A **table** is a piece of furniture with legs and a flat top.

Another word that sounds like **tail** is **tale**.

tail

A **tail** is the part of an animal that grows out of the back end of its body. Airplanes also have **tails**.

tale

A **tale** is a story. *Do you know the tale of Cinderella and her fairy godmother?*

Another word that sounds like **tale** is **tail**.

talk (talking, talked)

When you **talk**, you say words. *My little sister can't talk yet because she is only a baby.*

tall

Somebody or something that is **tall** goes up a long way from the ground. *There are a lot of tall buildings in a city.*

tame

A **tame** animal is not wild or afraid of people. *Pets are tame animals.*

tap (tapping, tapped)

When you **tap** something, you hit it, but not very hard.

taste

1 (tasting, tasted) When you **taste** food, you put it in your mouth to see what it is like. *You taste food with your tongue.*
2 A **taste** is what food or drink is like in your mouth. *I don't like the taste of lemons.*

taught Look at **teach**.

tea

Tea is a drink that is made by adding boiling water to the dried leaves of special plants. *Would you like a cup of tea?*

teach (teaches, teaching, taught)

You **teach** somebody by helping them to learn something or by showing them how to do something. *My mom is teaching me to use a computer.*

teacher

A **teacher** is somebody who teaches something, usually in a school. *Mrs. Smith is our teacher.*

team

A **team** is a group of people who play a game together on the same side. *There are five players on a basketball team.*

tear *rhymes with *here

A **tear** is a drop of water that comes from your eye when you cry.

tear *rhymes with *hair
(tearing, tore, torn)

When you **tear** something, you pull it apart.

Sarah is tearing the piece of paper in half.

teeth Look at **tooth**.

telephone

You use a **telephone** for talking to people who are far away. *The telephone rang but nobody answered it.*

telescope

You use a **telescope** for looking at things that are far away and making them look bigger and closer.

television

A **television** is an instrument that picks up waves sent through the air and turns them into sounds and pictures. *I sometimes watch television when I get home from school.* The short name for **television** is **TV**.

tell (telling, told)

If you **tell** somebody about something, you say what you know about it. *Please could you tell me how to open this box?*

temperature

The **temperature** of something is how hot or cold it is. **Temperature** is measured in numbers called degrees.

tent

A **tent** is a place to sleep in that is made of cloth and held up by poles and ropes. *Going camping and staying in a tent is very exciting.*

terrible

Something that is **terrible** is very, very bad. *The weather is **terrible**—it has been raining all day.*

test

A **test** is a way of finding out how much somebody knows about something. *We had a spelling **test** at school today.*

thank

When you **thank** someone, you tell them you are glad about something they did or said. ***Thank** you for the birthday present.*

theater

A **theater** is a place where people go to see plays or movies.

thick

1 Something that is **thick** measures a lot from one side to the other. *Castles have very **thick** walls.*
2 Liquids that are **thick** do not flow easily. *Honey is a **thick** liquid.*

thin (thinner, thinnest)

1 If something is **thin**, it is not very far between the two sides. *The pages of this dictionary are **thin**.*
2 **Thin** also means not fat.

think (thinking, thought)

When you **think**, you have ideas in your head. ***Think** carefully before you answer this question.*

third

Third means next after the second one. *Hannah came first in the race, Paul came second, and I came **third**.*

thirsty

When you are **thirsty**, you want something to drink. *I was so **thirsty** that I drank three glasses of water.*

thought

1 A **thought** is an idea. *Have you had any **thoughts** about what you would like to do this afternoon?*
2 Look at **think**.

thread

Thread is a very thin string of material like cotton or wool. *People use a needle and **thread** to sew.*

threw Look at **throw**.

Another word that sounds like **threw** is **through**.

throat

Your **throat** is the part at the back of your mouth. *I have a sore **throat**.*

through

Through means from one side to the other. *We crawled **through** a hole in the fence.*

Another word that sounds like **through** is **threw**.

throw

(throwing, threw, thrown)

When you **throw** something, you make it move through the air using your hand.

*Levi has **thrown** the ball into the air.*

thumb

Your **thumb** is the short, fat finger nearest your wrist.

thunder

Thunder is the loud noise that you hear in the sky after a flash of lightning. You hear **thunder** when there is a **thunderstorm**.

ticket

A **ticket** is a small piece of paper that shows that you have paid for something. *You have to have a **ticket** to travel on the train. My mom bought **tickets** for the movie.*

tie

1 (tying, tied) When you **tie** something, you hold it together with something like string or ribbon.

*Alice is **tying** her shoes.*

2 A **tie** is a long, thin piece of cloth that you can tie around the neck of a shirt so that it hangs down the front.

tiger

A **tiger** is a big, wild cat with orange fur and black stripes. **Tigers** live in Asia.

tight

If something is **tight**, it is not loose or easy to take off. *These shoes are too **tight** for me—my feet are hurting.*

time

Time is when something happens. We measure **time** in years, months, weeks, days, hours, minutes, and seconds. *"What **time** is it?" "It's two o'clock."*

tiny (tinier, tiniest)

Something that is **tiny** is very small. *The magician had a toy pigeon dressed in a **tiny** suit of clothes with a **tiny** hat.*

tire

A **tire** is a circle made of rubber that covers the outside of a wheel.

tired

When you are **tired**, you feel that you want to rest or to go to sleep. *Mom felt **tired** so she went to bed early.*

toad

A **toad** is an animal that looks like a large frog. *I saw a **toad** by the edge of the pond.*

toe

Your **toes** are the five parts that you have at the end of each foot.

together

Together means with each other. *My friend and I always walk to school **together**.*

told Look at **tell**.

tomato (tomatoes)

A **tomato** is a soft, round, red fruit that is used to make foods like soup and ketchup.

tongue

Your **tongue** is the long, pink part inside your mouth. Your **tongue** helps you to taste, to swallow food, and to speak.

tool

A **tool** is something that we use to help us do work. *A hammer is a **tool** that is used for hitting nails into things.*

tooth (teeth)

A **tooth** is one of the hard, white parts inside your mouth. We bite and chew food with our **teeth**.

top

1 The **top** of something is the highest part.

*The cat climbed to the **top** of the tree.*

2 A **top** is something that covers a thing like a bottle or a jar. *Don't forget to put the **top** back on the tube of toothpaste.*

tore Look at **tear**.

torn Look at **tear**.

tornado

A **tornado** is a storm with strong winds that spin around in a circle. *We could see the **tornado** go right by the town.*

touch (touches, touching, touched)

1 If you **touch** something, you put your hand on it and feel it. *Don't **touch** the iron—it's very hot!*

2 If two things are **touching**, there is no space between them. *Jonjo and Felicity sat close together with their backs **touching**.*

toward

Toward means in the direction of something. *My dog ran **toward** me.*

towel

A **towel** is a large piece of cloth you use to dry yourself.

town

A **town** is a place where there are a lot of streets, houses, stores, and other buildings. A **town** is bigger than a village.

toy (toys)

A **toy** is something you can play with. *We made the kitten a **toy** out of string.*

trace (tracing, traced)

When you **trace** a picture, you put a thin piece of paper over it and then draw over the lines of the picture to copy it.

tractor

A **tractor** is a strong machine with big wheels. Farmers use **tractors** for pulling heavy things.

traffic

Traffic is all the cars, buses, vans, and trucks moving along the road. *At some times of the day there is a lot of **traffic**.*

traffic lights

Traffic lights are a set of red, yellow, and green lights by the road that tell drivers when to stop and go.

train

1 A **train** is something that you can travel in. It is pulled by an engine along a railroad. ***Trains** stop at stations.*

2 (training, trained) To **train** a person or an animal is to teach them how to do something. *Some dogs have been **trained** to help blind people.*

trap

A **trap** is something that is used to catch an animal or a person. *They set a **trap** to catch the rat.*

travel (traveling, traveled)

When you **travel**, you go from one place to another. *We **traveled** to my aunt and uncle's house by train.*

treasure

Treasure is a big pile of things like gold, silver, and jewels. *The pirates hid their **treasure** in a cave.*

tree

A **tree** is a plant with branches, leaves, and a thick stem, called a trunk, made of wood. *Many **trees** can grow to be very tall.*

triangle

A **triangle** is a shape with three straight sides.

trick

1 A **trick** is a clever plan to make somebody believe something that is not true. *We played a **trick** on our teacher by hiding his books when he wasn't looking.*
2 A **trick** is also something that seems impossible. *The magician does card **tricks**.*

trip

1 A **trip** is when you travel somewhere. *We went on a school **trip** to the museum.*
2 (tripping, tripped) When you **trip**, you hit your foot against something and fall. *Put your toys away before somebody **trips** over them.*

trouble

If you have **trouble** doing something, there are problems. *The woman in the library had a lot of **trouble** finding the book I wanted.*

trousers

Trousers are something that you wear. They cover your legs and bottom.

truck

A **truck** is a big, motor vehicle for carrying things. *My aunt is a **truck** driver.*

true

1 If something is **true**, it really happened. *Is that a **true** story?*
2 **True** also means right. *It is **true** that the Earth is round.*

trumpet

A **trumpet** is a musical instrument that you play by blowing into it.

trunk

1 The **trunk** of a tree is the thick, round part that grows up from the ground.
2 An elephant's **trunk** is its long nose, which it uses to lift food and water.
3 A **trunk** is also a large box, or space in a car, for keeping things in.

trust (trusting, trusted)

If you **trust** somebody, you know they will do what they promise. *Mrs. Wilson **trusted** Alice to look after the younger children.*

truth

The **truth** is what is true. *You should always tell the **truth**.*

try (tries, trying, tried)

1 When you **try** to do something, you do your best to do it. *I **tried** to fix my bicycle, but I couldn't.*
2 To **try** also means to do or taste something to see if you like it. *Have you **tried** this chocolate drink? It's delicious!*

tub

A **tub** is a wide, round container for bathing in or for keeping things in.

tube

A **tube** is a long, hollow thing like a pipe made of plastic, metal, rubber, or glass.

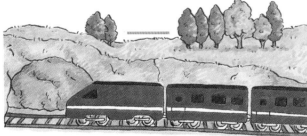

tunnel

A **tunnel** is a long hole through a hill or under the ground. *The train went through a **tunnel** in the mountains.*

turn (turning, turned)

1 When something **turns**, it moves around. *The wheels of a bike **turn** when you push the pedals.*
2 When something **turns** into another thing, it changes into that thing. *Water **turns** into ice when it freezes.*

twin

Twins are two children who have the same mother and father, and who were born at the same time. Some **twins** look exactly alike.

*Sometimes I can't tell the difference between David and Richard because they are **twins**.*

twist (twisting, twisted)

If you **twist** something, you turn it around and around. *I **twisted** the wires together.*

tying Look at **tie**.

161

ugly (uglier, ugliest)

Somebody or something that is **ugly** is not nice to look at. *Pretend you are a monster and make an **ugly** face.*

umbrella

An **umbrella** is a thing that you hold over you to stay dry when it rains. It is made of a round piece of cloth joined to a long handle.

uncle

Your **uncle** is the brother of your father or your mother, or the husband of your aunt.

under

1 Under means lower than the bottom of something. *The dog is hiding **under** the chair.*
2 Under also means covered by something. *A plant's roots grow **under** the ground.*

understand (understanding, understood)

If you **understand** something, you know what it means. *Do you **understand** all the words on this page?*

undress (undressing, undressed)

When you **undress**, you take off your clothes. *You get dressed in the morning and you **undress** at night.*

unhappy (unhappier, unhappiest)

If you are **unhappy**, you are sad. *Nicky was **unhappy** when her dog ran away.*

uniform

A **uniform** is a set of special clothes that people wear to show they belong to the same group. *Nurses, the police, and people who work in restaurants wear **uniforms**.*

universe

The **universe** is the Earth, the Sun, the Moon and all the other planets and stars. *The Earth is only a very tiny dot in the **universe**.*

until

Until means up to a certain time. *I go to school every day from nine o'clock **until** three o'clock.*

unusual

Something that is **unusual** is not usual. *It is unusual to see a cat without a tail.*

up

If somebody or something goes **up**, it moves from a lower place to a higher place. *It's hard work riding up the hill.*

upset

When you are **upset**, you feel unhappy. *Bobby was upset when he lost his balloon.*

upside down

If something is **upside down**, the bottom is at the top and the top is at the bottom.

*The letter "u" on Mia's shirt is **upside down**.*

upstairs

Upstairs means to a higher part of a building. *I am going upstairs to bed now.*

urgent

If something is **urgent**, it must be done right away.

use (using, used)

When you **use** something, you do a job with it. *You use a ruler for measuring and drawing straight lines.*

useful

If something is **useful**, it helps you in some way. *An umbrella is useful when it rains.*

usual

Something is **usual** if it happens most of the time. *Today I got up at eight o'clock as usual.*

usually

Usually means almost always. *The weather is usually cold in winter.*

Wordplay

Copy this list of words onto a piece of paper. Then close your dictionary and see how quickly you can put them in alphabetical order.

usually upset unusual usual understand undress

If the second letter of the words is the same, look at the third letter and so on.

Answer at the back!

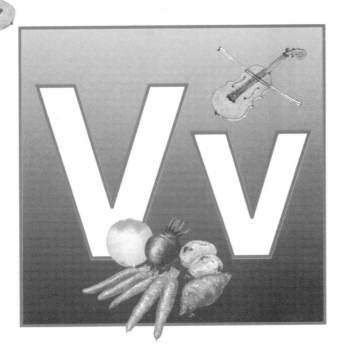

valley (valleys)

A **valley** is low land between hills. *Many valleys have rivers flowing through them.*

van

A **van** is a small covered truck used for carrying things.

vanish (vanishes, vanishing, vanished)

If something **vanishes**, it goes away suddenly. *We watched the plane until it vanished above the clouds.*

vase

A **vase** is something that you fill with water and put flowers in.

vegetable

A **vegetable** is a part of plant that people eat. *Carrots and potatoes are vegetables.*

vet

A **vet** is a kind of doctor who looks after animals that are sick or hurt.

video

A **video** is a special kind of tape that records and stores pictures and sound. You play it on a **video** recorder.

village

A **village** is a small group of houses and other buildings. **Villages** are smaller than towns and they are usually in the country.

violin

A **violin** is a musical instrument made of wood. You hold it under your chin and move a stick called a bow across it to play it.

visit (visiting, visited)

If you **visit** somebody or something, you go to see them. *Natasha visited her friend who was in the hospital.*

voice

Your **voice** is the sound that you make when you speak or sing. *I could hear voices outside my room.*

Vegetables

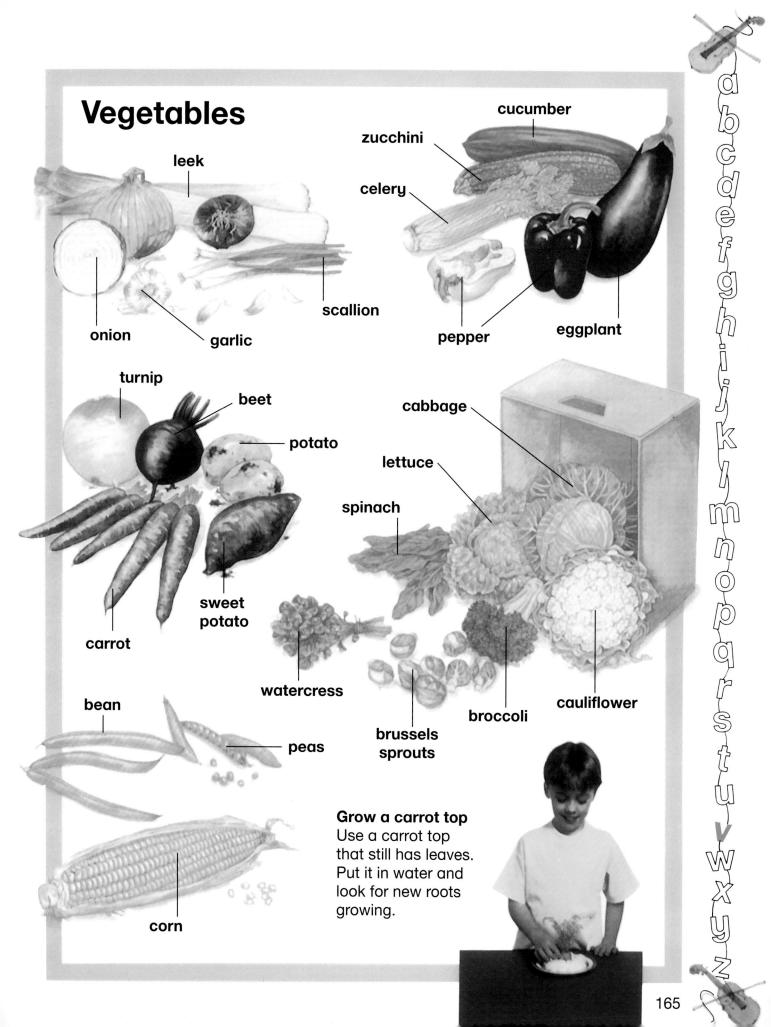

leek

cucumber

zucchini

celery

onion

garlic

scallion

pepper

eggplant

turnip

beet

potato

cabbage

lettuce

spinach

sweet potato

carrot

watercress

cauliflower

brussels sprouts

broccoli

bean

peas

Grow a carrot top
Use a carrot top that still has leaves. Put it in water and look for new roots growing.

corn

W w

wagon

A **wagon** is used to carry people and things from one place to another. A **wagon** has four wheels. Large **wagons** are pulled by horses.

wait (waiting, waited)

If you **wait**, you stay where you are because you are expecting something to happen.

*We **waited** for half an hour before the bus came.*

wake (waking, woke, woken)

When you **wake** up, you stop sleeping. *Please **wake** me up early tomorrow.*

walk (walking, walked)

When you **walk**, you move along on your feet. *I **walk** to school every day.*

wall

1 A **wall** is one of the sides of a building or of a room. *A room usually has four **walls**.*
2 A **wall** is also something made of bricks or stones that you can see around some fields and yards.

*Wendy is painting the **wall**.*

want (wanting, wanted)

When you **want** something, you would like to have it. *Do you **want** a drink?*

war

A **war** is a time when armies are fighting against each other.

Another word that sounds like **war** is **wore**.

warm

Warm means not cold but not very hot. *You wear gloves in winter to keep your hands **warm**.*

wash (washes, washing, washed)

When you **wash** something, you make it clean with soap and water. *Remember to **wash** your hands before you eat.*

wasp

A **wasp** is a flying insect with yellow and black stripes on its body. *Wasps can sting.*

waste (wasting, wasted)

If you **waste** something, you use more of it than you need. *You mustn't waste electricity by leaving all the lights on.*

watch

1 (watches, watching, watched) If you **watch** something, you look at it for a while. *Kim is watching television.*
2 (watches) A **watch** is a small clock that you wear around your wrist.

water

Water is the clear liquid that is in oceans, lakes, and rivers. *All living things need water.*

wave

1 A **wave** is a curved line of water moving across a sea.
2 (waving, waved) When you **wave**, you move your hand up and down to say hello or good-bye to somebody.

Jenna is waving to her friend.

wax

Wax is used to make candles and crayons. It gets soft and melts when it gets very hot.

way (ways)

1 A **way** of doing something is how you do it. *Do it the way I showed you.*
2 A **way** is also how you get from one place to another. *Can you tell me the way to the station, please?*

Another word that sounds like **way** is **weigh**.

weak

Somebody or something that is **weak** is not strong. *If you didn't eat or drink you would soon become very weak.*

Another word that sounds like **weak** is **week**.

wear (wearing, wore, worn)

1 When you **wear** clothes, you have them on your body. *Lola is wearing a red dress.*
2 When something **wears** out, it cannot be used any more.

I played my new game all week and the batteries wore out.

Another word that sounds like **wear** is **where**.

weather

The **weather** is how hot, cold, windy, rainy, or sunny it is outside. *What's the weather like today? We've had wet weather for two days.*

web

A **web** is a kind of net that a spider makes to catch insects to eat.

week

A **week** is seven days. *There are 52 weeks in a year.*

Another word that sounds like **week** is **weak**.

weigh (weighing, weighed)

You **weigh** something on a scale to find out how heavy it is. *Mia is weighing some bananas.*

Another word that sounds like **weigh** is **way**.

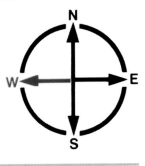

well (better, best)

1 When you do something **well**, you do it in a good way. *Paul plays the flute very well.*
2 If you are **well**, you are healthy. *I was sick last week but now I am well.*

west

The **west** is where the Sun goes down in the evening. The opposite direction is east.

wet (wetter, wettest)

Something that is **wet** is covered with water or full of water. *You will get wet if you go out in the rain.*

whale

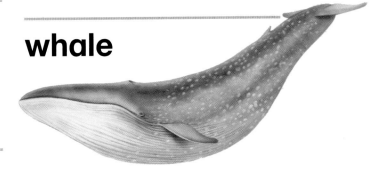

A **whale** is a very large animal that lives in the ocean. **Whales** look like fish but they are really mammals.

wheat

Wheat is a plant that farmers grow. We use its seeds, called grain, to make flour.

wheel

A **wheel** is a round thing. **Wheels** go around and around to move things along the ground. *Cars, trucks, and wheelchairs have wheels.*

whisper (whispering, whispered)

When you **whisper**, you speak very quietly. You **whisper** to somebody when you don't want other people to hear you.

whistle

1 (whistling, whistled) When you **whistle**, you make a musical sound by blowing air through your lips. *I **whistled** to my dog to make him come back.*
2 A **whistle** is a small instrument that makes a sound when you blow through it.

whole

The **whole** of something is all of it. *Wilf ate the **whole** cake—he didn't leave any.*

Another word that sounds like **whole** is **hole**.

wide

Something that is **wide** measures a lot from one side to the other. *The piano is too **wide** to fit through the door.*

wife (wives)

A man's **wife** is the woman he is married to.

wild

Wild animals and plants are animals and plants that are not looked after by people. *Squirrels are **wild** animals.*

win (winning, won)

When you **win** a game or a race, you finish first or do better than everybody else. *I **won** the 100-yard dash.*

wind

The **wind** is air that is moving very fast. *The **wind** blew the man's hat off.*

window

A **window** is a hole in the wall of a building that lets in light from outside. **Windows** usually have glass in them.

wing

Birds, bats, and some insects have **wings** that they use to fly. Airplanes also have **wings**.

winter

Winter is the coldest part of the year. **Winter** comes after autumn and before spring.

wire

A **wire** is a long, thin piece of metal that bends easily. *Electricity goes along **wires**.*

wish (wishes, wishing, wished)

If you **wish** for something, you want to have it or you want it to happen very much. *I **wish** I could fly.*

witch
(witches)

A **witch** is a person who is thought to have magic powers.

Another word that sounds like **witch** is **which**.

wives Look at **wife**.

wizard

A **wizard** is a person who is thought to have magic powers.

woke Look at **wake**.

woken Look at **wake**.

wolf (wolves)

A **wolf** is a wild animal that looks like a big dog with a pointed nose and pointed ears. A young **wolf** is called a cub.

woman (women)

A **woman** is a grown-up female person.

won

Look at **win**.

Another word that sounds like **won** is **one**.

wonder (wondering, wondered)

If you **wonder** about something, you think about something that you do not know the answer to. *I wonder why the Earth is round.*

wonderful

If something is **wonderful**, it is very good. *I like your picture. I think it's wonderful.*

wood

Wood is what trees are made of. People use **wood** to build houses.

woods

The **woods** is a place where many trees grow near each other.

Another word that sounds like **wood** is **would**.

wool

Wool is the soft, thick hair that grows on sheep. **Wool** is used for making cloth and for knitting. Sweaters and scarves are often made of **wool**.

word

We use **words** when we speak or write. **Words** are made of sounds or letters of the alphabet and each word means something.

wore Look at wear.

Another word that sounds like **wore** is **war**.

work

1 Work is what somebody does as a job, or something else that they have to do. *What time does your mom go to work?*
2 (working, worked) When you **work**, you do or make something. *Helen works in a bank.*
3 If a machine **works**, it does what it should do. *This clock doesn't work anymore.*

world

The **world** is the planet that we live on and all its countries and people. *What is the biggest city in the world?*

worm

A **worm** is a small creature with a long, thin body and no legs. *Many worms live in the ground.*

worn Look at wear.

worry (worries, worrying, worried)

If you **worry**, you keep thinking of bad things that might happen. *Mom worries when I'm late coming home from school.*

worse

Worse means more bad. *The weather was bad yesterday, but it's worse today.*

worst

Worst means most bad. *Can you remember the worst food you have ever eaten?*

wrap (wrapping, wrapped)

If you **wrap** something, you cover it with something else.

wrist

Your **wrist** is the thin part of your arm just above your hand.

write (writing, wrote, written)

When you **write**, you make words with a pen or pencil. *Milo is writing with his new pen.*

Another word that sounds like **write** is **right**.

wrong

Wrong means not right or not good. *It's wrong to say that six and two make nine. Stealing money is also wrong.*

wrote Look at write.

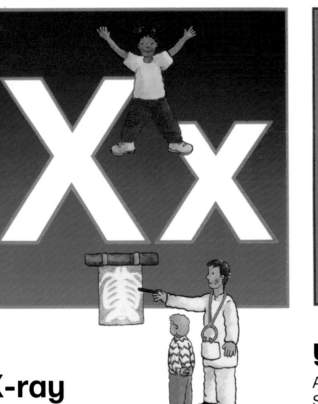

X-ray

An **X-ray** is a special kind of photograph that shows what the inside of your body looks like. *At the hospital the doctor showed me an **X-ray** of my chest.*

xylophone *say **zy**lofone

A **xylophone** is a musical instrument that is made of flat bars of different lengths. You play it by hitting these bars with small hammers to make music.

Wordplay
Do you know what the young of these animals are called? The dictionary explanations will help you.

goose   gosling

sheep

horse

Answers at the back!

wolf

yacht *rhymes with *got*

A **yacht** is a boat with sails or an engine. Some **yachts** are used for racing. *Last week my brother and I went sailing with my uncle on his **yacht**.*

yawn (yawning, yawned)

When you **yawn**, you open your mouth wide and breathe deeply. People **yawn** when they are tired.

*Rosa is **yawning**.*

year

A **year** is an amount of time. There are 12 months in one **year**.

yell (yelling, yelled)

If you **yell**, you shout. *"Come over here!" she **yelled**.*

yesterday

Yesterday means the day before today. *Today is Tuesday, so **yesterday** was Monday.*

yolk *say yoke

A **yolk** is the yellow part in the middle of an egg.

young

A person or an animal that is **young** has not been alive for very long. *Puppies are **young** dogs, and lambs are **young** sheep.*

zebra

A **zebra** is an animal that looks like a horse with black and white stripes on its body. **Zebras** live in Africa.

zero (zeros)

Zero is the number 0. *You write ten with a one and a **zero**.*

zigzag

A **zigzag** is a line that bends sharply up and down.

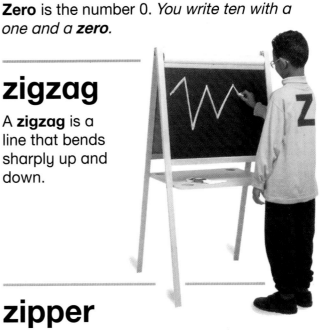

zipper

A **zipper** is a long metal or plastic thing that holds together two edges of material. Pants and jackets often have **zippers**.

zoo

A **zoo** is a place where wild animals are kept so that people can go to look at them.

More about words

Naming, Counting, and Measuring Things

Days
Monday
Tuesday
Wednesday
Thursday
Friday
Saturday
Sunday

Months
January
February
March
April
May
June
July
August
September
October
November
December

Numbers

1 one	first	
2 two	second	
3 three	third	
4 four	fourth	
5 five	fifth	
6 six	sixth	
7 seven	seventh	
8 eight	eighth	
9 nine	ninth	
10 ten	tenth	
11 eleven	eleventh	
12 twelve	twelfth	
13 thirteen	thirteenth	
14 fourteen	fourteenth	
15 fifteen	fifteenth	
16 sixteen	sixteenth	
17 seventeen	seventeenth	
18 eighteen	eighteenth	
19 nineteen	nineteenth	
20 twenty	twentieth	
30 thirty	thirtieth	
40 forty	fortieth	
50 fifty	fiftieth	
60 sixty	sixtieth	
70 seventy	seventieth	
80 eighty	eightieth	
90 ninety	ninetieth	
100 one hundred	one hundredth	
1,000 one thousand	one thousandth	

Money
1 penny = 1 cent
a nickel = 5 cents
a dime = 10 cents
a quarter = 25 cents
a half dollar = 50 cents
one dollar = 100 cents

Distance
12 inches = 1 foot
3 feet = 1 yard
5,280 feet = 1 mile

10 millimeters = 1 centimeter
100 centimeters = 1 meter
1,000 meters = 1 kilometer

Weight
16 ounces = 1 pound
2,000 pounds = 1 ton

1,000 grams = 1 kilogram

Liquids
8 ounces = 1 cup
2 cups = 1 pint
2 pints = 1 quart
4 quarts = 1 gallon

Kinds of Words

Noun

A **noun** is a word that names a person, place, or thing. The words *alphabet, finger, helmet, library, promise,* and *truth* are all **nouns**.

Pronoun

A **pronoun** is a word used in place of a noun or a name. In the first sentence below, *moon* is a noun. In the second sentence, the word *it* is a **pronoun** used in place of the word *moon*. *Did you see the **moon** tonight? **It** is very bright.*

The **pronouns** below are called **personal pronouns** because they tell us what person or thing is being talked about. *I think **you** can do it by **yourself**.*

The **personal pronouns** are:

I, me, myself   it, itself
you, yourself   we, us, ourselves
he, him, himself   you, yourselves
she, her, herself   they, them, themselves

Some **pronouns**, called **possessive pronouns**, tell who or what something belongs to. *These are **our** books. The dictionary is **hers**. The tree has lost **its** leaves.*

The **possessive pronouns** are:

my, mine   its
your, yours   our, ours
his   your, yours
her, hers   their, theirs

This and *these* are **pronouns** used to talk about a person, thing, or group that is near you. *That* and *those* are **pronouns** used to talk about a person, thing, or group that is farther away. ***These** are my shoes and **those** are my brother's.*

Some **pronouns** can be used when you mean any person or thing in a group: *any, anybody, anyone, anything, everybody, everyone, everything, somebody, someone, something, few, none, no one.*

The **pronouns** *what, which, who,* and *whose* are used when asking questions or when you want to say more about something.
***Who** are you? **Whose** is this? She is the girl **who** saved my life.*

Verb

A **verb** is a word that tells the action of a sentence. *Walk, run, tell, use,* and *worry* are **verbs** in your dictionary.

Some other common **verbs** are:

be (*am, are, is, was, were, being, been*)
become (*becoming, became*)
can (*could*)
come (*coming, came*)
do (*does, doing, did, done*)
get (*getting, got, gotten*)
go (*goes, going, went, gone*)
happen (*happening, happened*)
have (*has, having, had*)

let (*letting, let*)
look (*looking, looked*)
make (*making, made*)
may (*might*)
must
put (*putting, put*)
shall (*should*)
take (*taking, took, taken*)
will (*would*)

Helping verb

Some verbs are called **helping verbs**, because they help another verb in the sentence. **Helping verbs** often give information about when the action of the verb takes place.

Some common **helping verbs** are:

be: *He **is** coming now. We **are** leaving soon. She has **been** trying to find it.*

will: *Jorge **will** bring the dessert. I **would** like to go now.*

can: *You **can** see for miles. Philip **could** play the piano.*

have: *Nadine **has** arrived. They **have** left already. He **had** forgotten his shoes.*

may: ***May** we go now? You **might** see me there.*

must: *You **must** tell the truth.*

shall: ***Shall** we dance? I **should** leave soon.*

will: *Mother **will** take you to the train. I **would** like to see you.*

Contraction

A **contraction** is a shortened form of a two-word phrase. In **contractions**, the mark **'**, called an **apostrophe**, takes the place of a sound that is not pronounced. When the words *did* and *not* make a **contraction**, the *o* of *not* is not pronounced. The **contraction** of *did not* is *didn't.* The **contraction** of *will not* is unusual; it is *won't.*

Here are some more **contractions**:

-n't = not	***-'d*** = would or had
aren't	I'd
can't	you'd
couldn't	he'd
didn't	she'd
doesn't	we'd
don't	they'd
hadn't	
haven't	
isn't	***-'ll*** = will
mustn't	I'll
shouldn't	you'll
wasn't	he'll
weren't	she'll
won't	we'll
wouldn't	they'll

-'m = am	***-'ve*** = have
I'm	I've
	you've
	we've
-'re = are	they've
you're	
they're	
we're	

-'s = is
he's
she's
it's

Adjective

An **adjective** is a word that tells you something more about a noun or pronoun. Some **adjectives** in your dictionary are *afraid, easy, expensive, heavy, noisy, pure, ripe,* and *smooth.*

Some common **adjectives** are used in the sentences below:

either: *You can use **either** hand.*
every: *I get taller **every** day.*
few: *She caught a **few** fish.*
neither: ***Neither** man knew the answer.*
other: *Her **other** sister is not home.*
less: *I drink **less** milk than you.*
least: *What is the **least** amount of money you will earn?*

many: *She was born **many** years ago.*
more: *Three **more** people came today.*
most: ***Most** children go to school.*
much: *This is taking too **much** time.*
some: ***Some** animals make good pets.*
such: *I never heard **such** nonsense before.*
which: ***Which** hat should I wear?*
whose: ***Whose** coat is this?*

Adverb

An **adverb** is a word that tells you something about a verb, an adjective, or even another **adverb**. **Adverbs** ask or answer questions like *How? When? Where?* and *How much?*

How?: **How** did you find out? We ran **quickly**. Andrei had a cold, but he went to school **anyway**.

When?: **When** did she leave? We are going home **today**. **Sometimes** I feel sad. I am happy **now**. Did you **ever** meet her? Alexa has **just** left.

Where?: Let's go **there** now! I lost my watch **somewhere**. Ann will meet you **here** at two o'clock. We are moving **away** next month.

How much?: Are you feeling **any** better? There is **no** music lesson this week. You are making **too** much noise!

Here are some **adverbs** that are used often:

above	away	no	sometimes	too
ago	below	not	somewhere	very
already	else	now	still	well
also	ever	nowhere	then	when
any	everywhere	perhaps	there	where
anyway	here	probably	today	why
anywhere	how	so	tomorrow	yes
as	just	some	tonight	yet

Preposition

A **preposition** is a word that describes the position of something, as in the following sentences:

*The money is **in** the box. Grass grows **around** the house. The tunnel goes **under** the river. He was leaning **against** a tree. I'm not **at** home. She got **off** her bike. The principal **of** our school is very fair. He came **with** me.*

Some common **prepositions** are:

about	*by*	*in*	*off*	*over*	*until*
against	*down*	*into*	*on*	*through*	*up*
around	*for*	*near*	*onto*	*to*	*upon*
at	*from*	*of*	*out*	*under*	*with*

Conjunction

A **conjunction** is a word that joins two sentences or two parts of a sentence together.

Some common **conjunctions** are:

and   as   but   if   or   than

*My brother is in the fourth grade **and** my sister is in the sixth grade.*

*I like swimming **and** football.*

*She fell down **but** didn't hurt herself.*

*I will come **if** my mom lets me.*

*She played the piano **as** I sang.*

Article

An **article** is a word that signals that a noun will follow. There are three **articles**, *a*, *an*, and *the*.

*This is **a** book.*

*He ate **an** orange.*

*Look at **the** sky.*

Wordplay answers

Page 7
ball, call, fall, hall, tall, wall

Page 11
A ladybug is an insect.
A swallow is a bird.
A snake is a reptile.
A seahorse is a fish.
A tree frog is an amphibian.
An elephant is a mammal.

Page 17
bear/bare
son/sun
nose/knows
two/too
I/eye
meet/meat
see/sea
pair/pear

Page 24
branch, birthday, bud, beetle,
bubble

If you take the third letter of
each of these words and mix
them up, they spell "beard."

Page 32
foot/feet
woman/women
mouse/mice
calf/calves
city/cities

Page 39
cat, crocodile, chicken, calf,
camel, caterpillar

Page 49

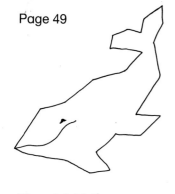

It's a dolphin!

Page 50
draw, raw, wing, in

Page 54
plane, cube, hope, bare, kite

Page 61
feet, few, fine, fire, fireworks,
first, fist, fit, foot, for, forest,
fork, free, front, frost, frown
(Maybe you found more that
aren't in the dictionary!)

Page 71
The message says: Well done.

Page 83
There are eight: cap, jeans,
glove, belt, scarf, pants,
shoe, sock.

Page 86
1 car, key, wheel
2 powder, pretty, puppy
3 tractor, triangle, true

Page 92
live (it becomes "evil" when
you spell it backward). The
other words are: wolf (flow),
net (ten), pot (top).
Did you think of any more?

Page 99
If you hold the message up to
a mirror, you should be able
to read:

> What
> keys are
> furry?
> Monkeys!

Page 105

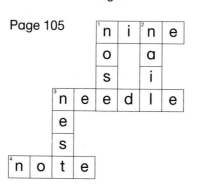

Page 117
bread, pizza, potato, cheese

Page 128
tail/tale
way/weigh
hole/whole
dear/deer
plane/plain

Page 132
sandwich (sand + witch!)
butterfly (butter + fly)
rainbow (rain + bow)
lighthouse (light + house)

Page 146
balloon, scissors, pencil,
giraffe, iron

Page 153
sheep, ant, swan, zebra, bat,
snake, owl, rat, panda

Page 163
understand, undress,
unusual, upset, usual, usually

Page 172
goose/gosling
sheep/lamb
horse/foal
wolf/cub